Ngondro for Our Current Day

Ngondro for Our Current Day

A Short Ngondro Practice and Its Instructions
by the Gyalwang Karmapa Ogyen Trinley Dorje

Root text translated by Tyler Dewar.
Instructions and other materials translated by David Karma Choephel.

KTD Publications
Woodstock New York

Published by: KTD Publications
Karma Triyana Dharmachakra
335 Meads Mountain Road
Woodstock, NY 12498, USA
www.KTDPublications.org

ISBN 978-1-934608-16-6

Front cover drawing by Sergey Noskow
Back cover photo by by Pema Oser Dorje, 2009
Vajradhara and Vajrasattva line drawings by Sange Wangchuk
from the collection of Michael and Margaret Erlewine

Printed in Canada on acid-free, 100% PCR paper.

Contents

Translator's Introduction

David Karma Choephel

In recent years, more people in developed countries have developed the wish to do the special preliminary practices for mahamudra meditation. Yet the traditional ngondro practice—which Tibetans generally practice in the confines of a retreat—is hard for many people to fit into their lives, as the text is relatively long and reciting it in Tibetan can be daunting even with a transliteration.

For this reason among others, in 2006 the Seventeenth Gyalwang Karmapa Ogyen Trinley Dorje composed a new short ngondro practice specifically for students from developed countries. The text is shorter so that it will be easier for people with jobs and busy lives to incorporate into their schedule, and the Gyalwang Karmapa said that people may also do the practice in their own language. In December of 2006, His Holiness gave instructions on this new short preliminary practice to a group of students from East Asian and Western countries at Tergar Monastery in Bodhgaya, India.

This book includes all the materials a student will need to do this practice, including the Short Vajradhara Lineage Prayer, verses on the four common preliminaries, His Holiness' *Brief Recitations for the Four Preliminary Practices*, and the instructions the Gyalwang Karmapa gave. The translation of the root text was prepared, based on earlier translations, by Tyler Dewar for His Holiness' visit to the United States in 2008. The text of the instructions is a translation of a transcript of the Tibetan-language teachings in December of 2006. It was transcribed, edited, and published by Drophen Tsuklak Petunkhang, the publishing arm of the Tsurphu Labrang, in 2008.

However, this book is not a substitute for oral instructions from a qualified master. Because His Holiness the Karmapa had only four days to teach these practices, he had to omit many details and did not explain the postmeditation practice. For this reason, anyone wishing to do the practice included in this book should first receive the reading transmission (*lung*) and then ask an experienced lama for instructions and guidance. In particular, His Holiness asked that cameras and other recording devices be turned off during the teachings on guru yoga, and thus this book does not include any instructions on guru yoga. In order to practice guru yoga one will need to make a connection with a living master and receive the proper guidance.

I would like to thank the following people and organizations for their assistance in preparing this translation: the Tsurphu Labrang and Drophen Tsuklak Petunkhang; Ringu Tulku Rinpoche; Khenpo Lodrö Tengye and Cheng Sheng Publications from Taiwan for their assistance in comparing this translation against the Chinese; Lhundup Damchö for editing; and Tyler Dewar for his assistance and gracious permission to use his translation of the root text.

The Short Mahamudra Ngondro Practice

The Short Vajradhara Lineage Prayer

By Pengar Jampal Sangpo

རྡོ་རྗེ་འཆང་ཆེན་ཏེ་ལོ་ནཱ་རོ་དང་། །
མར་པ་མི་ལ་ཆོས་རྗེ་སྒམ་པོ་པ། །
དུས་གསུམ་ཤེས་བྱ་ཀུན་མཁྱེན་ཀར་མ་པ། །
ཆེ་བཞི་ཆུང་བརྒྱད་བརྒྱུད་པར་འཛིན་རྣམས་དང་། །
འབྲི་སྟག་ཚལ་གསུམ་དཔལ་ལྡན་འབྲུག་པ་སོགས། །

dor je chang chen te lo na ro dang
mar pa mi la chö je gam po pa
dü sum she ja kün khyen kar ma pa
che shi chung gye gyü par dzin nam dang
dri tak tsal sum pal den druk pa sok

Great Vajradhara, Telo, Naropa,
Marpa, Mila, Dharma Lord Gampopa,
The knower of three times, omniscient Karmapa,
Those who hold the four elder and eight younger lineages,
The Drikung and Taklung and Tsalpa, great Drukpa,

ཟབ་ལམ་ཕྱག་རྒྱ་ཆེ་ལ་མངའ་བརྙེས་པའི། །

མཉམ་མེད་འགྲོ་མགོན་དྭགས་པོ་བཀའ་བརྒྱུད་ལ། །

གསོལ་བ་འདེབས་སོ་བཀའ་བརྒྱུད་བླ་མ་རྣམས། །

བརྒྱུད་པ་འཛིན་ནོ་རྣམ་ཐར་བྱིན་གྱིས་རློབས། །

sap lam chak gya che la nga nye pay
nyam me dro gön dak po ka gyü la
sol wa dep so ka gyü la ma nam
gyü pa dzin no nam tar jin gyi lop

And others who've mastered mahamudra's profound path,
Unequaled protectors of beings, Dakpo Kagyu,
We supplicate you. Kagyu gurus, we uphold
Your lineage: Please bless us to follow your example.

ཞེན་ལོག་སྒོམ་གྱི་རྐང་པར་གསུངས་པ་བཞིན། །

ཟས་ནོར་ཀུན་ལ་ཆགས་ཞེན་མེད་པ་དང་། །

ཚེ་འདིའི་གདོས་ཐག་ཆོད་པའི་སྒོམ་ཆེན་ལ། །

རྙེད་བཀུར་ཞེན་པ་མེད་པར་བྱིན་གྱིས་རློབས། །

shen lok gom gyi kang par sung pa shin
se nor kün la chak shen me pa dang
tse diy dö tak chö pay gom chen la
nye kur shen pa me par jin gyi lop

Detachment's the foot of meditation, as it's taught.
As ones with no craving for food or for wealth,
Who cut all the ties to this life: Please bless us
To have no attachment to honor or to gain.

མོས་གུས་སྐྱོམ་གྱི་མགོ་བོར་གསུངས་པ་བཞིན། །

མན་ངག་གཏེར་སྒོ་འབྱེད་པའི་བླ་མ་ལ། །

རྒྱུན་དུ་གསོལ་བ་འདེབས་པའི་སྐྱོམ་ཆེན་ལ། །

བཅོས་མིན་མོས་གུས་སྐྱེ་བར་བྱིན་གྱིས་རློབས། །

mö gü gom gyi go wor sung pa shin

men ngak ter go che pay la ma la

gyün du sol wa dep pay gom chen la

chö min mö gü kye war jin gyi lop

Devotion's the head of meditation, as it's taught.

As ones who pray always to the lama who opens

The gate to the treasury of oral instructions:

Please bless us to develop genuine devotion.

ཡེངས་མེད་སྒོམ་གྱི་དངོས་གཞིར་གསུངས་པ་བཞིན། །
གང་ཤར་རྟོག་པའི་ངོ་བོ་སོ་མ་དེ། །
མ་བཅོས་དེ་ཀར་འཇོག་པའི་སྒོམ་ཆེན་ལ། །
བསྒོམ་བྱ་བློ་དང་བྲལ་བར་བྱིན་གྱིས་རློབས། །

yeng me gom gyi ngö shir sung pa shin
gang shar tok pay ngo wo so ma de
ma chö de kar jok pay gom chen la
gom ja lo dang dral war jin gyi lop

The main practice is being undistracted, as it's taught.
As ones who whatever arises, rest simply,
Not altering, in just that fresh essence of thought:
Please bless us with practice that's free of conception.

རྣམ་རྟོག་ངོ་བོ་ཆོས་སྐུར་གསུངས་པ་བཞིན། །

ཅི་ཡང་མ་ཡིན་ཅིར་ཡང་འཆར་བ་ལ། །

མ་འགགས་རོལ་པར་འཆར་བའི་སྒོམ་ཆེན་ལ། །

འཁོར་འདས་དབྱེར་མེད་རྟོགས་པར་བྱིན་གྱིས་རློབས། །

nam tok ngo wo chö kur sung pa shin
chi yang ma yin chir yang char wa la
ma gak röl par char way gom chen la
khor de yer me tok par jin gyi lop

The essence of thought's the dharmakaya, as it's taught.
Not anything at all, yet arising as anything,
In unceasing play we arise: Please bless us
To realize samsara and nirvana inseparable.

སྐྱེ་བ་ཀུན་ཏུ་ཡང་དག་བླ་མ་དང་། །

འབྲལ་མེད་ཆོས་ཀྱི་དཔལ་ལ་ལོངས་སྤྱོད་ཅིང་། །

ས་དང་ལམ་གྱི་ཡོན་ཏན་རབ་རྫོགས་ནས། །

རྡོ་རྗེ་འཆང་གི་གོ་འཕང་མྱུར་ཐོབ་ཤོག །

ཅེས་པའང་བེན་སྒར་བ་འཇམ་དཔལ་བཟང་པོས་མཛད་པའོ།། །།

kye wa kün tu yang dak la ma dang

dral me chö kyi pal la long chö ching

sa dang lam gyi yön ten rap dzok ne

dor je chang gi go pang nyur top shok

In all of our births may we never be separate
From the perfect guru, enjoying dharma's splendor.
Perfecting the qualities of the paths and levels,
May quickly we reach the state of Vajradhara.

Composed by Pengar Jampel Sangpo.

The Four Ordinary Foundations

Extracted from the Daily Recitation of the Mahamudra Preliminaries
by the Ninth Karmapa, Wangchuk Dorje

The Precious Human Body

དང་པོ་བསྒོམ་བྱ་དལ་འབྱོར་རིན་ཆེན་འདི། །
ཐོབ་དཀའ་འཇིག་སླ་ད་རེས་དོན་ཡོད་བྱ། །

dang po gom ja dal jor rin chen di
top ka jik la da re dön yö ja

First meditate on this precious human body,
So hard to attain and easy to lose.
I shall make this life meaningful!

གཉིས་པ་སྣོད་བཅུད་ཐམས་ཅད་མི་རྟག་ཅིང་། །
སྣོས་སུ་འགྲོ་བའི་ཚེ་སྲོག་ཆུ་བུར་འདྲ། །
ནམ་འཆི་ཆ་མེད་ཤི་ཚེ་རོ་རུ་འགྱུར། །
དེ་ལ་ཆོས་ཀྱི་ཕན་ཕྱིར་བརྩོན་པས་བསྒྲུབ། །

nyi pa nö chü tam che mi tak ching
gö su dro way tse sok chu bur dra
nam chi cha me shi tse ro ru gyur
de la chö kyi pen chir tsön pay drup

Second, the world and living beings are impermanent.
Our lives in particular are like water bubbles—
Who knows when we will die and become corpses?
Since Dharma will help then, I'll practice diligently.

གསུམ་པ་ཤི་ཚེ་རང་དབང་མི་འདུ་བར། །
ལས་ནི་བདག་གིར་བྱ་ཕྱིར་སྡིག་པ་སྤངས། །
དགེ་བའི་བྱ་བས་རྟག་ཏུ་འདའ་བར་བྱ། །
ཞེས་བསམ་ཉིན་རེ་རང་རྒྱུད་ཉིད་ལ་བརྟག །

sum pa shi tse rang wang mi du war
le ni dak gir ja chir dik pa pang
ge way ja way tak tu da war ja
she sam nyin re rang gyü nyi la tak

Third, there is no freedom at the time of death.
In order to take control over karma,
I give up misdeeds and always do virtuous acts.
Thinking thus, I examine myself every day.

བཞི་པ་འཁོར་བའི་གནས་གྲོགས་བདེ་འབྱོར་སོགས། །

སྡུག་བསྔལ་གསུམ་གྱིས་རྟག་ཏུ་མནར་བའི་ཕྱིར། །

གསོད་སར་ཁྲིད་པའི་གཤེད་མའི་དགའ་སྟོན་ལྟར། །

ཞེན་འཕྲེས་བཅད་ནས་བརྩོན་པས་བྱང་ཆུབ་སྒྲུབས། །

shi pa khor way ne drok de jor sok
duk ngel sum gyi tak tu nar way chir
sö sar tri pay she may ga tön tar
shen tri che ne tsön pay jang chup drup

Fourth, the places, friends, pleasures, and riches of samsara,
Are always stricken with the three sufferings;
They're like a feast before being led to execution.
Cutting the ties of attachment, I'll strive and reach enlightenment.

ༀ། །སྟོན་འགྲོ་བཞི་སྦྱོར་གྱི་ངག་འདོན་མདོར་བསྡུས་བཞུགས་སོ། །

Brief Recitations for the Four Preliminary Practices

By the Seventeenth Karmapa Ogyen Trinley Dorje

དཔལ་ལྡན་ཁྱབ་བདག་རྡོ་རྗེ་འཆང་དབང་རིགས་ཀུན་གཙོ་བོ་བླ་མ་ཀརྨ་པ། །
དཀྱིལ་འཁོར་ཀུན་གྱི་འབྱུང་གནས་སྲིད་ཞིའི་དཔལ་གྱུར་ཡི་དམ་རྡོ་རྗེ་རྣལ་
འབྱོར་མ། །ཕྲིན་ལས་ཀུན་གྱི་བྱེད་པོར་དབང་བསྒྱུར་ཆོས་སྐྱོང་བེར་ཅན་ལྕམ་
དྲལ་ལ། །རྣལ་འབྱོར་རྩེ་གཅིག་གུས་པས་འདུད་དོ་འབྲལ་མེད་ཕྱགས་རྗེས་སྐྱོང་
བར་མཛོད། །

Glorious, powerful, omnipresent Lord Vajradhara, principal of all
  Buddha families—Guru Karmapa,
Origin of all mandalas, glory of samsara and nirvana—Yidam
  Vajrayogini,
Those who have power over enlightened activity—dharma protectors
  Bernakchen and consort,
This yogi bows to you with one-pointed respect—please protect me
  forever with your noble compassion.

འདིར་གང་ཟག་གང་ཞིག་ལམ་ཐུན་མོང་བས་རྒྱུད་སྦྱངས་པ་སྟོན་དུ་སོང་བས། ཆོས་སྐྱོན་གྱི་བླ་མའི་དྲུང་ནས་དབང་དང་གདམས་པ་ལེགས་པར་ཞུས་ཏེ། ཕྱག་ཆེན་གྱི་ཐུན་མིན་སྟོན་འགྲོའི་འདོན་སྒོམ་བགྱི་བ་ལ།

Once individuals have purified their mindstreams with the common preliminary practices, they should excellently request empowerment and instruction from a qualified guru and then train in the recitation meditation of Mahamudra's extraordinary preliminary practices as follows.

སྐྱབས་འགྲོ་སེམས་བསྐྱེད།

Going for Refuge and Giving Rise to Bodhichitta

ཐོག་མར་ཅི་བྱེད་ཆོས་སུ་འགྲོ་བ་སྐྱབས་འགྲོ་སེམས་བསྐྱེད་ལ། ཐུན་དང་ཐུན་མཚམས་གཉིས་ལས། དང་པོ་ནི་འཇིག་

རྟེན་དང་བྱ་བ་གཞན་གྱི་སྐྱོས་པ་བཅད་དེ་བདེ་བའི་སྟན་ལ་ལུས་གནད་གཙུན་ཏེ།

First, so that everything you do will accord with the dharma, go for refuge and give rise
to bodhichitta in two ways: during meditation sessions and in between meditation sessions. During meditation sessions, leave worldly concerns and other activities aside, sit
in a proper meditation posture on a comfortable seat, and recite:

རང་མདུན་ནམ་མཁར་བླ་མ་རྡོ་རྗེ་འཆང་། །

དེ་ལ་དོན་བརྒྱུད་བྱིན་རླབས་བརྒྱུད་པ་དང་། །

ཆོས་འབྲེལ་དད་ཐོབ་བླ་མའི་ཚོགས་ཀྱིས་བསྐོར། །

མདུན་དུ་ཡི་དམ་གཡས་སུ་སངས་རྒྱས་དང་། །

རྒྱབ་ཏུ་དམ་ཆོས་གཡོན་དུ་དགེ་འདུན་བཅས། །

rang dün nam khar la ma dor je chang
de la dön gyü jin lap gyü pa dang
chö drel de top la may tsok kyi kor
dün du yi dam ye su sang gye dang
gyap tu dam chö yön du gen dün che

Before me in the sky is the Guru Vajradhara,
Surrounded by the gurus of the lineage of meaning and blessings
And gurus with whom I have dharmic connections of faith.
In front are the yidams, to the right are the buddhas.
Behind is the sacred dharma; to the left, the sangha.

རང་རང་རིགས་མཐུན་འཁོར་ཚོགས་རྒྱ་མཚོས་བསྐོར། །

སྐྱབས་ཡུལ་ཀུན་གྱི་སྤྱན་ལམ་འོག་ཕྱོགས་སུ། །

མ་གྱུར་སེམས་ཅན་ཀུན་ཀྱང་འཁོད་གྱུར་པས། །

རྩེ་གཅིག་ཡིད་ཀྱིས་སྐྱབས་འགྲོ་སེམས་བསྐྱེད་གྱུར། །

rang rang rik tün khor tsok gya tsoy kor
kyap yul kün gyi chen lam ok chok su
ma gyur sem chen kün kyang khö gyur pay
tse chik yi kyi kyap dro sem kye gyur

All are surrounded by ocean-like retinues of their own kind.
My mothers, sentient beings, and I stand together
As the sources of refuge gaze down upon us.
One-pointedly, we go for refuge and arouse bodhichitta.

བདག་དང་སེམས་ཅན་ཐམས་ཅད་བླ་མ་ལ་སྐྱབས་སུ་མཆིའོ། །

ཡི་དམ་ལྷ་ལ་སྐྱབས་སུ་མཆིའོ། །

སངས་རྒྱས་ལ་སྐྱབས་སུ་མཆིའོ། །

ཆོས་ལ་སྐྱབས་སུ་མཆིའོ། །

དགེ་འདུན་ལ་སྐྱབས་སུ་མཆིའོ། །

dak dang sem chen tam che la ma la kyap su chi o
yi dam lha la kyap su chi o
sang gye la la kyap su chi o
chö la kyap su chi o
gen dün la kyap su chi o

All sentient beings and I go for refuge to the gurus.
We go for refuge to the yidams.
We go for refuge to the buddhas.
We go for refuge to the dharma.
We go for refuge to the sangha.

དགོན་མཆོག་རིགས་ལྔར་སྐྱབས་སུ་འགྲོ་བ་ཅི་ནུས་དང་། དམིགས་པ་དེ་ཉིད་ཀྱི་སྤྱུས་སུ་མཐུད་དེ་སེམས་བསྐྱེད་བྱ་བ་ནི།

བྱང་ཆུབ་སྙིང་པོར་མཆིས་ཀྱི་བར། །

སངས་རྒྱས་རྣམས་ལ་སྐྱབས་སུ་མཆི། །

ཆོས་དང་བྱང་ཆུབ་སེམས་དཔའ་ཡི། །

ཚོགས་ལའང་དེ་བཞིན་སྐྱབས་སུ་མཆི། །

jang chup nying por chi kyi bar
sang gye nam la kyab su chi
chö dang jang chup sem pa yi
tsok la'ang de shin kyab su chi

Go to these five jewels for refuge as many times as possible. Maintaining the same visualization, arouse bodhichitta:

Until I reach enlightenment's essence,
I go for refuge to the buddhas.
To the dharma and the assembly
Of bodhisattvas, too, I go for refuge.

ཇི་ལྟར་སྟོན་གྱི་བདེ་གཤེགས་ཀྱིས། །

བྱང་ཆུབ་ཐུགས་ནི་བསྐྱེད་པ་དང་། །

བྱང་ཆུབ་སེམས་དཔའི་བསླབ་པ་ལ། །

དེ་དག་རིམ་བཞིན་གནས་པ་ལྟར། །

ji tar ngön gyi de shek kyi
jang chup tuk ni kye pa dang
jang chup sem pay lap pa la
de dak rim shin ne pa tar

Just as the sugatas of the past
Aroused the mind of bodhichitta;
Just as they followed step-by-step
The training of the bodhisattvas,

དེ་བཞིན་འགྲོ་ལ་ཕན་དོན་དུ། །
བྱང་ཆུབ་སེམས་ནི་བསྐྱེད་བགྱི་ཞིང་། །
དེ་བཞིན་དུ་ནི་བསླབ་པ་ལའང་། །
རིམ་པ་བཞིན་དུ་བསླབ་པར་བགྱི། །ལན་གསུམ།

de shin dro la pen dön du
jang chup sem ni kye gyi shing
de shin du ni lap pa la'ang
rim pa shin du lap par gyi (3x)

So, too, shall I, to benefit wanderers
Arouse the mind of bodhichitta.
So, too, shall I follow step-by-step,
The bodhisattva's training.
Recite three times.

བྱང་ཆུབ་སེམས་མཆོག་རིན་པོ་ཆེ། །

མ་སྐྱེས་པ་རྣམས་སྐྱེ་གྱུར་ཅིག །

སྐྱེས་པ་ཉམས་པ་མེད་པ་དང་། །

གོང་ནས་གོང་དུ་འཕེལ་བར་ཤོག །

jang chup sem chok rin po che
ma kye pa nam kye gyur chik
kye pa nyam pa me pa dang
gong ne gong du pel war shok

Then recite the following:
May precious and supreme bodhichitta
Arise where it has not arisen,
Not diminish where it has arisen,
And continually increase and increase.

མཐར་མར་སྐྱབས་ཡུལ་འོད་ཞུ་བདག་དང་འདྲེས།

གཉིས་པ་ཐུན་མཚམས་སུ། །རང་རྒྱུད་བཏང་སྙོམས་སུ་མ་ལུས་པར། གཉེན་པོས་བཟུང་སྟེ། བླ་མ་ལ་མོས་གུས་དེ་ཆེ། གོན་མཆོག་ལ་དད་པ་ཅི་སྐྱེ། སེམས་ཅན་ལ་སྙིང་རྗེ་དེ་སྐྱེད་ལ་འབད་དགོས་པ་ཡིན་ནོ། །

Finally, the sources of refuge melt into light and then become one with me.

Second, between sessions, do not be indifferent. Take up the antidotes: Strive to increase devotion to the guru, to develop as much faith in the rare and supreme jewels as possible, and to have greater and greater compassion for sentient beings.

རྡོར་སེམས་སྒོམ་བཟླས།

Vajrasattva Meditation and Recitation

༔ ཕྱག་རྐྱེན་དག་པར་ཕྱེད་པ་རྡོར་སེམས་སྒོམ་བཟླས་ལ་གཉིས་ལས། དང་པོ་ནི།

རང་གི་སྤྱི་བོར་པད་ཟླའི་གདན་གྱི་སྟེང་། །

བླ་མ་རྡོ་རྗེ་སེམས་དཔའ་རྒྱུན་ཕྱུན་དཀར། །

ཞལ་གཅིག་ཕྱག་གཉིས་གཡས་པས་རྡོ་རྗེ་དང་། །

གཡོན་པས་དྲིལ་བུ་འཛིན་ཅིང་སྐྱིལ་ཀྲུང་བཞུགས། །

rang gi chi wor pe day den gyi teng

la ma dor je sem pa gyen den kar

shal chik chak nyi ye pay dor je dang

yön pay dril bu dzin ching kyil trung shuk

The Vajrasattva meditation and recitation practice, which purifies negativity and obscurations, has two parts. First, during meditation sessions, recite:

Above the crown of my head, on a lotus-moon seat,
Is Guru Vajrasattva, white in color, adorned with ornaments,
With one face and two arms,
Holding a vajra with his right hand and a bell with his left, and
   seated in vajra posture.

ཐུགས་ཀར་ཟླ་དཀྱིལ་ལ་ཧཱུྃ་དང་སྔགས་ཕྲེང་བཞག་པ་གསལ་བར་དམིགས་ནས་གསོལ་བ་བཏབ་པས་བདུད་རྩིའི་རྒྱུན་
སྐུ་ལས་བརྒྱུད་དེ་ཞབས་གཡས་པའི་མཐེ་བོང་ནས་བབས། རང་གི་ཚངས་བུག་ནས་མར་ཞུགས། སྡིག་སྒྲིབ་ཐམས་
ཅད་སྨག་ཚོམ་དུད་ཁུ་བ་ལྟ་བུར་དོན་ལུས་ཐམས་ཅད་བདུད་རྩིའི་རྒྱུན་དེས་གང་བ་ལ་སེམས་གཏད་དེ།

Clearly visualize at Vajrasattva's heart center a moon disc, upon which sits a HUM, *encircled by the mantra garland. Due to your supplicating him, a stream of amrita fills his body and descends from his right big toe, entering the Brahma aperture at the top of your head. All your obscurations and past negative actions, embodied in a substance that looks like ink or dark smoke, leave your body as all of your body's parts are filled with amrita. While doing this visualization, recite Vajrasattva's mantra as many times as you can:*

ༀ་བཛྲ་སཏྭ་ས་མ་ཡ་མ་ནུ་པཱ་ལ་ཡ། །བཛྲ་སཏྭ་ཏྭེ་ནོ་པ་ཏིཥྛ། ཌྲི་ཌྷོ་མེ་བྷ་བ། སུ་ ཏོཥྱོ་མེ་བྷ་བ། སུ་པོཥྱོ་མེ་བྷ་བ། ཨ་ནུ་རཀྟོ་མེ་བྷ་བ། སརྦ་སིདྡྷི་མེ་པྲ་ཡ་ཙྪ། སརྦ་ཀརྨ་སུ་ཙ་མེ་ཙིཏྟཾ་ཤྲེ་ཡཿ་ཀུ་རུ་ཧཱུྃ། ཧ་ཧ་ཧ་ཧོཿ བྷ་ག་བཱན་སརྦ་ཏ་ཐཱ་ག་ ཏ། བཛྲ་མཱ་མེ་མུཉྩ། བཛྲི་བྷ་བ། མ་ཧཱ་ས་མ་ཡ་སཏྭ་ཨཱཿ ༀ་བཛྲ་སཏྭ་ཧཱུྃ། །ཞེས་ གྱུང་ཅི་ནུས་བཟྡ་དོ།

OM VAJRASATTVA SAMAYAM ANUPĀLAYA VAJRASATTVA TVENOPATIṢṬHA

DRIDHO ME BHAVA SUTOṢHYO ME BHAVA SUPOṢHYO ME BHAVA

ANURAKTO ME BHAVA SARVA-SIDDHI ME PRAYACCHA SARVA-KARMASU CHA

ME CHITTAM SHREYAḤ KURU HŪM HA HA HA HA HOḤ BHAGAVAN SARVA-

TATHĀGATA VAJRA MĀ ME MUÑCHA VAJRĪ BHAVA MAHĀSAMAYASATTVA AḤ

OM VAJRASATTVA HŪM

Then, confess your past negative actions and vow not to perform them again by reciting the following:

ཐམས་ཅད་མཁྱེན་གཟིགས་ལྷ་རྣམས་དགོངས་སུ་གསོལ། །

ཐོག་མ་མེད་པའི་དུས་ནས་བདག་ཅག་གིས། །

དུག་གསུམ་དབང་གིས་ལུས་ངག་ཡིད་གསུམ་གྱིས། །

སྡོམ་གསུམ་རྒྱལ་བའི་བཀའ་ལས་འདས་གྱུར་པ། །

ཉེས་ལྟུང་སྡིག་པའི་ལས་བགྱིས་མཐོལ་ལོ་བཤགས། །

ལྷན་ཆད་མི་བགྱིད་སྡོང་བར་མ་གྱུར་ཅིག །

ཞེས་སོགས་བཤགས་བསྡམ་བྱ། རྡོ་རྗེ་སེམས་དཔས་ཀྱང་རྣམ་པར་དག་གོ་ཞེས་དགྱེས་པར་མཛད་ཅིང་འོད་དུ་ཞུ་བ་རང་ལ་བསྟིམས་ནས་མཉམ་པར་བཞག །

tam che khyen sik lha nam gong su söl
tok ma me pay dü ne dak chak gi
duk sum wang gi lü ngak yi sum gyi
dom sum gyal way ka le de gyur pa
nye tung dik pay le gyi tol lo shak
len che mi gyi nyong war ma gyur chik

Noble ones who know and see everything, think of us.

Since beginningless time,

Under the power of the three poisons,

We have transgressed the three vows and the victors' commands

In body, speech, and mind.

We admit and confess these downfalls and misdeeds

And promise not to do them again—may we not experience

   their results.

Saying this, confess and resolve not to repeat your misdeeds. Vajrasattva says, "Your misdeeds are purified," and is pleased. He melts into light and dissolves into you. Rest in equipoise.

གཉིས་པ་ནི། ཉོན་མོངས་དང་རྣམ་རྟོག་ཅི་ཤར་ཡང་། ཤར་མ་ཐག་ཏུ་དྲན་པས་བཟུང་ནས་འཕྲོ་ཐད་བཅད་ནས་འཛིན་མེད་ཀྱི་རང་དུ་བཞག །སེམས་ཅན་གང་མཐོང་ཐོས་དྲན་གསུམ་བྱུང་རིགས་དང་། ལྷག་པར་སྡིག་པོ་ཆེ་ལ་དམིགས་ནས་རྡོར་སེམས་སྤྱི་བོར་བསྒོམ་ཞིང་ཡིག་བརྒྱ་བརྗོད་དོ། །

Second, between sessions: whatever afflictions or thoughts arise, be mindful of them as soon as they arise. Completely cut through them and rest in freedom from fixation. Whatever sentient beings you see, hear, or think of—especially those who have done terrible misdeeds—visualize Vajrasattva above their heads and recite the hundred-syllable mantra.

ཚོགས་གསོག་མཎྜལ།

The Mandala Offering,
Which Gathers the Two Accumulations

༄། ཚོགས་གཉིས་རྫོགས་པར་བྱེད་པ་མཎྜལ་གྱི་ཚོག་ལ་གཉིས་ལས། དངོས་ནི། ཞིང་གཙོ་བོར་གྱུར་པ་སྒྲུབ་པའི་མཎྜལ། དངོས་པོ་གཙོ་བོར་གྱུར་པ་མཆོད་པའི་མཎྜལ་གཉིས་ལས་དངོས་ནི། མཎྜལ་གྱི་གཞི་གང་ཡང་རུང་བར་ཕྱོགས་བཞིར་དབུས་དང་ལྔར། པདྨའི་སྡོང་པོ་རེ་རེར་སེང་གེ་བརྒྱད་ཀྱིས་བཏེགས་པའི་རིན་པོ་ཆེའི་ཁྲི་པདྨ་ཉི་ཟླའི་སྟེང་དུ། དབུས་སུ་བླ་མ། མདུན་དུ་ཡི་དམ། གཡས་སུ་སངས་རྒྱས། རྒྱབ་ཏུ་ཆོས། གཡོན་དུ་དགེ་འདུན་དཀོན་མཆོག་རྣམས་དང་། མཐར་དམ་པའི་ཆོས་སྐྱོང་བ་དང་བཅས་པ་དམིགས་ལ། དོན་དུན་བཞིན་པས་ཡན་ལག་བདུན་པ་ཡང་འབུལ་ཏེ།

The mandala ritual, which completes the two accumulations, has two parts. First, during meditation sessions, there are two types of mandalas: the mandala of accomplishment, the field of focus for one's gathering of the two accumulations, and the offering mandala, which contains the substances offered. For the first of these, the mandala's physical base may be made of any suitable material. Visualize that in its center and each of its four directions there are lotus flowers, upon each of which stand eight lions supporting a throne made of precious jewels, upon which is a lotus, sun, and moon seat. On these central thrones sit the gurus, in front sit the yidams, to the right the buddhas, behind the dharma, and to the left the sangha—so are the rare and supreme jewels arrayed. The dharma protectors guard the mandala's perimeter. While remembering its meaning, offer the seven branches:

འོག་མིན་ཆོས་ཀྱི་དབྱིངས་ཀྱི་ཕོ་བྲང་དུ། །
དུས་གསུམ་སངས་རྒྱས་ཀུན་གྱི་ངོ་བོ་ཉིད། །
རང་སེམས་ཆོས་སྐུར་མངོན་སུམ་སྟོན་མཛད་པའི། །
དཔལ་ལྡན་བླ་མ་དམ་པ་ལ་ཕྱག་འཚལ། །

---

ok min chö kyi ying kyi po drang du
dü sum sang gye kün gyi ngo wo nyi
rang sem chö kur ngön sum tön dze pay
pal den la ma dam pa la chak tsal

In the dharma expanse palace of Akanishtha
Is the essence of all buddhas of the three times,
Who directly shows my mind as dharmakaya:
I prostrate to the genuine, glorious guru.

ལུས་དང་ལོངས་སྤྱོད་ཡིད་ཀྱིས་སྤྲུལ་པ་ཡི། །
མཆོད་པ་ཀུན་གྱིས་མཆོད་ཅིང་བསྟོད་པར་བགྱི། །
སྔར་བྱས་སྡིག་པ་མ་ལུས་བཤགས་པར་བྱ། །
སྡིག་པ་གཞན་ཡང་ལེན་ཆད་མི་བགྱིད་དོ། །

lü dang long chö yi kyi trul pa yi
chö pa kün gyi chö ching tö par gyi
ngar che dik pa ma lü shak par ja
dik pa shen yang le che mi gyi do

My body, possessions, and all the pleasing things I can imagine,
I offer you; I praise you.
I confess all the misdeeds I have performed
And will never do such things again.

འགྲོ་ཀུན་དགེ་བ་ཀུན་ལ་རྗེས་ཡི་རང་། །

བྱང་ཆུབ་མཆོག་གི་རྒྱུར་ནི་བསྔོ་བར་བགྱི། །

མྱ་ངན་མི་འདའ་བཞུགས་པར་གསོལ་བ་འདེབས། །

ཐེག་མཆོག་བླ་མེད་ཆོས་འཁོར་བསྐོར་བར་བསྐུལ། །

dro kün ge wa kün la je yi rang

jang chup chok gi gyur ni ngo war gyi

nya ngen mi da shuk par sol wa dep

tek chok la me chö khor kor war kul

I rejoice in all sentient beings' virtuous actions.

I dedicate all this as a cause of supreme enlightenment.

I supplicate you to remain and not pass into nirvana.

Please turn the dharma wheel of the unsurpassably supreme vehicle.

བྱམས་དང་སྙིང་རྗེ་ཕྱོགས་མེད་འབྱོང་པ་དང་། །

དོན་དམ་ལྷན་ཅིག་སྐྱེས་པའི་ཡེ་ཤེས་དེ། །

རྒྱལ་བ་སྲས་བཅས་རྣམས་ཀྱིས་རྟོགས་པ་ལྟར། །

བདག་གིས་མངོན་སུམ་རྟོགས་པར་བྱིན་གྱིས་རློབས། །

jam dang nying je chok me jong pa dang
dön dam lhen chik kye pay ye she de
gyal wa se che nam kyi tok pa tar
dak gi ngön sum tok par jin gyi lop

Just as the victors and their heirs mastered
Universal love and compassion, and realized
The ultimate co-emergent wisdom,
Bless me that I may directly realize that.

མཆོད་པའི་མཎྜལ་འབུལ་བ་ནི།

ས་གཞི་སྤོས་ཆུས་བྱུགས་ཤིང་མེ་ཏོག་བཀྲམ། །

རི་རབ་གླིང་བཞི་ཉི་ཟླས་བརྒྱན་པ་འདི། །

སངས་རྒྱས་ཞིང་དུ་དམིགས་ཏེ་ཕུལ་བ་ཡིས། །

འགྲོ་ཀུན་རྣམ་དག་ཞིང་ལ་སྤྱོད་པར་ཤོག །

ཨི་དཾ་གུ་རུ་རཏྣ་མཎྜལ་ཀཾ་ནིརྻཱ་ཏ་ཡཱ་མི།

sa shi pö chü juk shing me tok tram

ri rap ling shi nyi day gyen pa di

sang gye shing du mik te pul wa yi

dro kün nam dak shing la chö par shok

IDAṂ GURU RATNA MAṆḌALA KAṂ NIRYĀTAYĀMI

Next, pick up the offering mandala and recite:

The earth is perfumed with scented water and strewn with flowers,
Adorned with Mount Meru, the four continents, sun, and moon.
Visualizing this as the buddha realm, I offer it
So that all beings may enjoy this perfectly pure realm.
IDAM GURU RATNA MANDALA KAM NIRYĀTAYĀMI

ཞེས་མཚལ་འདོན་སྐྱོམ་སྔགས་པ་བློ་ལ་རྣམ་པ་གསལ་པོར་མ་ནར་གྱི་བར་དུ་འབུལ། མཐར་མཚོད་ཡུལ་སོགས་ལ་
འཁོར་གསུམ་གྱི་རྟོག་པ་མེད་པར་མཉམ་པར་བཞག །

གཉིས་པ་ནི། རང་འདོད་ཀྱི་འཕྲི་བ་སྤངས་ནས་སྐོ་གསུམ་བླ་མ་དང་དཀོན་མཆོག་ལ་འབུལ། ཁྱད་པར་སྐྱབས་གནས་
དེ་དག་གི་རྟེན་ལ་ཞི་ཞུ་དང་རིམ་གྲོ་སོགས་བྱའོ། །

Combine the mandala recitation and meditation and offer the mandala until your visualization of it is vivid. Finally, rest in equipoise, free of thoughts of the offering's three spheres.

Second, in between meditation sessions, abandon self-centered attachment and offer your three gates to the guru and the rare and supreme jewels. Especially, offer respect, service, and veneration to these sources of refuge and their symbolic representations.

བླ་མའི་རྣལ་འབྱོར།
Guru Yoga

བྱིན་རླབས་མྱུར་དུ་འཇུག་པར་བྱེད་པ་བླ་མའི་རྣལ་འབྱོར་ལ་གཉིས་ལས། དང་པོ་ནི། ཐུན་མོན་དང་ཐུན་མོང་གཉིས་ལས་འདིར་ཐྱི་མ་ལྟར་སྒོམ་ན། རང་ཡི་དམ་གྱི་ལྟར་མོས་ཏེ།

Guru yoga, which quickly brings blessings, has two parts. First, during meditation sessions, there are the common and the extraordinary ways to do this practice. Here, do the former by visualizing yourself as your yidam and then reciting:

སྤྱི་བོར་པདྨ་ཉི་ཟླའི་གདན་སྟེང་དུ། །

རྩ་བའི་བླ་མ་རྡོ་རྗེ་འཆང་དབང་པོ། །

སྔོ་བསངས་རྡོར་དྲིལ་འཛིན་པའི་ཕྱག་རྒྱ་བསྣོལ། །

རིན་ཆེན་རྒྱན་མཛེས་མཚན་དཔེ་རབ་ཏུ་འབར། །

ཕྱོགས་དུས་རྒྱལ་ཀུན་འདུས་པའི་ངོ་བོར་གསལ། །

chi wor pe ma nyi day den teng du
tsa way la ma dor je chang wang po
ngo sang dor dril dzin pay chak gya nöl
rin chen gyen dze tsen pe rap tu bar
chok dü gyal kün dü pay ngo wor sal

Above the crown of my head, on a lotus, sun, and moon seat,
Is my root guru, the mighty Vajradhara,
Sky-blue, holding vajra and bell in his crossed arms,
Beautified by precious ornaments, blazing with major and minor marks,
The vivid embodiment of all ten directions and three times' victorious ones.

ཡན་ལག་བདུན་པ་གོང་བཞིན་ལ།

མ་ནམ་མཁའ་དང་མཉམ་པའི་སེམས་ཅན་ཐམས་ཅད་བླ་མ་སངས་རྒྱས་རིན་པོ་
ཆེ་ལ་གསོལ་བ་འདེབས་སོ། །

མ་ནམ་མཁའ་དང་མཉམ་པའི་སེམས་ཅན་ཐམས་ཅད་བླ་མ་ཀུན་ཁྱབ་ཆོས་ཀྱི་
སྐུ་ལ་གསོལ་བ་འདེབས་སོ། །

ma nam kha dang nyam pay sem chen tam che la ma sang gye
   rin po che la sol wa dep so
ma nam kha dang nyam pay sem chen tam che la ma kün khyap
   chö kyi ku la sol wa dep so

Recite the seven-branch prayer as above and then the supplication of the four kayas:
I and all my mother sentient beings, as great in number as space is vast,
supplicate the guru, the precious buddha.
I and all my mother sentient beings, as great in number as space is vast,
supplicate the guru, all-pervading dharmakaya.

མ་ནམ་མཁའ་དང་མཉམ་པའི་སེམས་ཅན་ཐམས་ཅད་བླ་མ་བདེ་ཆེན་ལོངས་

སྤྱོད་རྫོགས་པའི་སྐུ་ལ་གསོལ་བ་འདེབས་སོ། །

མ་ནམ་མཁའ་དང་མཉམ་པའི་སེམས་ཅན་ཐམས་ཅད་བླ་མ་ཐུགས་རྗེ་སྤྲུལ་

པའི་སྐུ་ལ་གསོལ་བ་འདེབས་སོ། །སྐུ་བཞི་མ་དང་།

ma nam kha dang nyam pay sem chen tam che la ma de chen long
   chö dzok pay ku la sol wa dep so
ma nam kha dang nyam pay sem chen tam che la ma tuk je trul
   pay ku la sol wa dep so

I and all my mother sentient beings, as great in number as space is vast,
supplicate the guru, great bliss sambhogakaya.
I and all my mother sentient beings, as great in number as space is vast,
supplicate the guru, great compassionate nirmanakaya.

Then, recite:

བླ་མ་རིན་པོ་ཆེ། །

དོན་གྱི་བརྒྱུད་པ་ཅན། །

བྱིན་རླབས་ཀྱི་འཕོ་བ་མཁན། །

རྟོགས་པའི་གདེང་ཚད་ཅན། །

la ma rin po che
dön gyi gyü pa chen
jin lap kyi po wa khen
tok pay deng tse chen

Precious guru
Who holds the lineage of meaning,
Who gives us blessings,
Who has the confidence of realization.

མངོན་ཤེས་སྤྱན་དང་ལྡན་པ། །
རྫུ་འཕྲུལ་བཀོད་པ་བསྟན་ཏེ། །
བཟོད་མེད་བཀའ་དྲིན་སྩོལ་བ། །
སངས་རྒྱས་ལག་བཅངས་སུ་གཏོད་པ། །
ཐ་མལ་སྣང་བ་བསྒྱུར་ཏེ། །

ngön she chen dang den pa
dzu trul kö pa ten te
sö me ka drin tsol wa
sang gye lak chang su tö pa
ta mal nang wa gyur te

Who has the clairvoyances and eyes,
Who shows arrays of miracles,
Who gives unbearable kindness,
Who places buddhahood in our palms,
Who transforms ordinary appearances

དག་པ་རབ་འབྱམས་སྟོན་པ། །

འཕགས་པ་འཇིག་རྟེན་དབང་ཕྱུག །

སྙིང་ཁོང་རུས་པའི་གཏིང་ནས། །

གཅིག་ཐུབ་གསོལ་བ་འདེབས་སོ། །

ཐུགས་རྗེས་འཛིན་པར་ཞུ་དང་། །

dak pa rap jam tön pa
pak pa jik ten wang chuk
nying khong rü pay ting ne
chik tup sol wa dep so
tuk je dzin par shu dang

And shows infinite purity,
You are the noble Lokeshvara.
From the depths of my heart,
I supplicate you, the all-capable.
Please hold me with your compassion.

དངོས་གྲུབ་ཀྱི་མཚན་ཁ་ཅན། །
བགའ་བརྒྱུད་རྩོད་པ་མེད་པ། །
དམུ་རྒོད་འདུལ་བའི་ནུས་པ། །
འཕྲིན་ལས་འགྲན་ཟླ་བྲལ་བ། །
རྫོགས་པའི་སངས་རྒྱས་དམ་པ། །

ngö drup kyi tsen kha chen
ka gyü tsö pa me pa
mu gö dul way nü pa
trin le dren da dral wa
dzog pay sang gye dam pa

The undisputed Kagyü lineage
Holds the power of the siddhis,
And can tame wild sentient beings—
Your enlightened activity is peerless.
You are the genuine and perfect Buddha.

སྒོ་གསུམ་དགེ་རྩ་དང་བཅས་པ། །

མཐའ་མེད་སེམས་ཅན་དོན་དུ། །

ད་ལྟ་ཉིད་དུ་འབུལ་ལོ། །

བརྩེ་བ་ཆེན་པོས་བཞེས་ཤིག །

བཞེས་ནས་འགྲོ་བ་ཀུན་གྱི། །

གཏན་སྐྱབས་ཐུབ་པའི་བླ་མ། །

རྗེ་བཙུན་ཁྱེད་རང་ལྟ་བུར། །

སྙིང་ནས་བྱིན་གྱིས་རློབས་ཤིག །

go sum ge tsa dang che pa

ta me sem chen dön du

da ta nyi du bül lo

tse wa chen poy she shik

she ne dro wa kün gyi

ten kyap tup pay la ma

je tsün khye rang ta bur

nying ne jin gyi lop shik

For the benefit of all the limitless sentient beings,
This very moment, I offer you
My body, speech, and mind, and all my roots of virtue.
Please accept them with your great love.
Having accepted them,
O lord and guru, ultimate protector
Of all wandering beings,
Please bless me that I might become like you.

གར་མ་ཕྲིན་དང་གཞན་ཡང་གསོལ་འདེབས་ཡུན་རིང་དུ་བྱ། བླ་མ་རྡོ་རྗེ་འཆང་རབ་ཏུ་དགྱེས་པའི་སྐུའི་གནས་གསུམ་ ལས་འོད་ཟེར་དཀར་དམར་མཐིང་གསུམ་འཕྲོས། རང་གི་སྒོ་གསུམ་གྱི་དྲི་མ་དག །དབང་བཞི་ཐོབ། སྐུ་བཞི་མངོན་དུ་ བྱས། མཐར་འོད་དུ་ཞུ་ནས་རང་ལ་ཐིམ་པས་བླ་མའི་སྐུ་གསུང་ཐུགས་དང་རང་གི་ལུས་ངག་ཡིད་གསུམ་དབྱེར་མེད་དུ་ གྱུར་པ་ལ་སེམས་བཞག་གོ །

Recite "*Karmapa, think of me*" (Karmapa Khyenno) *and other supplications at length. Visualize that the Guru Vajradhara is utterly pleased, and that from the three places on his enlightened form emanate white, red, and blue light respectively. These purify the stains of your own three gates, you receive the four empowerments, and you manifest the four kayas. Finally, the guru melts into light and dissolves into you. Rest in the equipoise of the guru's enlightened body, speech, and mind and your own body, speech, and mind being undifferentiable.*

གཉིས་པ་ནི། སྐྱོང་ལམ་ཐམས་ཅད་དུ་བླ་མའི་སྣང་བ་དང་མི་འབྲལ་བར་བྱ། སྐྱིད་སྡུག་ཐམས་ཅད་བླ་མའི་སྐུ་དྲིན་དུ་བལྟ་ ཞིང་། རྗེའི་བཞེད་པ་དང་རང་གི་འདོད་པ་རྒྱབ་འགལ་དུ་མ་སོང་བར་ཐུགས་ཡིད་གཅིག་འདྲེས་སུ་གྱོག་སྐྱམ་པའི་གསོལ་བ་ འཐབ་འཐབ་བཏྲེད། མདོར་ན་ཞི་སོགས་ཀྱི་ལས་གང་སྒྲུབ་ཀྱང་དམིགས་རྣམ་བསྐྱུར་བ་ཙམ་ལས་བླ་མ་ཉིད་ཀྱིས་ཆོག་པར་ བྱའོ། །

Second, in between meditation sessions, in all paths of conduct, never be apart from the appearance of the guru. View all happiness and suffering as the guru's kindness. Do not let your lord's intentions and your own desires contradict each other, but rather, pray again and again that his enlightened mind and your own mind will mix and become one. In short, whichever of the activities of pacifying and so forth you seek to accomplish, you need only to adjust your conduct's focus and the way you think of it and to supplicate the guru—that will suffice.

ཚུལ་འདི་རང་གི་འཕྲལ་མཁོར་རྗེ་ཤུ་དམར་ལུ་པའི་སྟོན་འགྲོའི་མན་ངག་དང་མཐུན་པར་ཀརྨ་པར་འབོད་པ། ཨོ་རྒྱན་ ཕྲིན་ལས་པས་སྟོད་རྒྱུད་གཙུག་ལག་ཁང་དུ་ཆུ་སྟོད་ཀྱི་ཉ་བའི་ཡར་ཚེས་དགུ་ལ་གྲུབ་པར་སྦྱར་བའོ། །༢༠༠༦ ༈ ༣

As it was needed quickly, the one called Karmapa, Ogyen Trinley, composed this according to the Fifth Shamar's pith instructions on the preliminaries on the ninth day of the waxing phase of the sixth Tibetan month at the temple of Gyutö, August 3, 2006

English translation compiled and revised by Tyler Dewar based upon previous translations by Ari Goldfield and Karma Choephel, April, 2008.

Instructions on the Four Special Preliminaries

Instructions on the Four Special Preliminaries

By the Seventeenth Karmapa Ogyen Trinley Dorje

This is a short teaching on the preliminaries for mahamudra practice. This preliminary or *ngondro* practice is different from the usual one. I wrote it because I needed to teach the preliminaries in four days, but that was not enough time to explain the usual ngondro practice. Thus from one perspective, I composed it because it was necessary for a particular teaching, but from another perspective, those of you who live in developed countries lead busy lives with a lot of work, which makes it difficult to do the longer preliminary practices. But doing your ngondro using this short ngondro practice will probably work out well.

However, Tibetans who are doing the preliminary practices do not have permission to use this text, even if they have received the transmission. This is because Tibetans like things easy, so when they see this short practice they will forget the long one. There is the danger the preliminaries will get shorter and shorter in the future. Thus Tibetans who want to do this short ngondro must ask for and receive special permission.

Common Preliminaries

There are many different types of individuals. There are some people who are able to practice mahamudra right from the start, but that is only so in the case of certain particular individuals. In terms of the general teachings or general path, whether we have sharp or dull faculties we first need to purify our beings through the general path by meditating on the four common preliminaries. Only after that should we begin the special mahamudra preliminaries. If we have not purified our minds through the common preliminaries and grasped the main points experientially, we will not get what we need out of the special preliminaries even if we do them. We will do them without getting them.

In some of the practice methods of the Kadampa masters of the past, people would meditate on impermanence until they developed a total experience of it within their beings. If they trained in impermanence in this life but did not come to such an experience, at the time of death they would make the aspiration to be able to continue that meditation and realize impermanence in their next life. Once they had an experience of impermanence, then they would begin the next contemplation. But in this context—whether or not you call it the mahamudra tradition—we first train our minds in the contemplation of, say, the precious human body so difficult to find. Even if that does not bring us to an experience of the preciousness of human life, that experience can come later when we meditate on impermanence. There are many different types of people. It is not absolutely necessary to force yourself to stick with one contemplation until you arrive at an experience of it.

In any case, you already have a bit of experience with the four common preliminaries. If there is one that you are more familiar with, practice that first. Once you are habituated to it, you will automatically be able to gain familiarity with the other common preliminaries, it is said. Similarly, it is not absolutely necessary that you go through them in a particular order, such as the precious human body first and then impermanence. It is fine to do the ones that are more familiar to you or easier for you to relate to, and then move on to the special preliminaries.

The text then says that individuals "should excellently request empowerment and instruction from a qualified guru…" The four special preliminary practices are a vajrayana practice. Vajrayana practices are not something that we study, contemplate, and meditate on our own. Without the support of a lama's blessings, we will be unable to develop an experience of a vajrayana practice. We can only receive a lama's blessings by following the tantras and the words of the Buddha. It is not okay to say, "I received blessings from some lama," and think that you have received blessings when there is no source or transmission. Thus we need to receive the empowerment from an authentic lama. In this context in particular, it should be the empowerment of either Chakrasamvara or Vajravarahi.

Similarly, it is also not okay to think that we can read books and figure out how great beings did their practices. There are many instructions from the lamas' experience that are not written in books—things we need to ask a lama about directly. This is why we need to receive the empowerments and instructions properly in the actual presence of a lama.

Refuge and Bodhichitta

The text continues, "During meditation sessions, leave worldly concerns and other activities aside…" I thought I would explain that briefly. Recently I have been extremely busy with the Kagyu Monlam, so much so that I think about work all the time and give myself headaches. Sometimes when I have to give an empowerment or teaching, I turn my attention inwards. But I start to think a little bit, and there is so much to do that my mind becomes busy and overactive. My thoughts seem intense and my mind gets agitated. When that happens, it is not easy to visualize or rest the mind steadily. Similarly, when you are at home in your own countries, all of you work and think so hard all day long that you give yourself headaches. In such a situation, I feel that it is probably extremely difficult to be able to practice the Dharma well.

So when I do my practice, I don't start meditating right away. First I relax my body and mind. This isn't a question of the Dharma, but of just relaxing. You should only begin to practice once you have become relaxed. Even if you do not practice a long time, you will be able to focus your mind a bit on whatever the object of the meditation is, and the stability and steadiness of your mind will be stronger.

Posture

You should find yourself a comfortable cushion. There are descriptions of a particular type of meditation cushion, but it would be very difficult for everyone to get such a cushion, so you should just get yourself a cushion that you find comfortable. A comfortable seat is important.

Generally, there are two ways of practicing meditation: we can practice primarily with our minds, or we can practice by using our body to influence our minds. For beginners, since it is easiest to use the body to hold the mind, you need to have good posture. The first point is the legs. The best posture is the vajra or full lotus position, which means to put each foot on top of the opposite thigh. The next best is the half-vajra posture, where you put your right foot on your left thigh. It is fine to sit in that posture as well. At the very least, you should relax and sit as we normally do, cross-legged on the floor.

Next are the hands: you should place your left hand below and your right hand on top with the tips of the two thumbs touching.

The main point is the spine. If your spine is hunched, your mind will become dull, which is a fault in shamatha meditation. If your spine is extended too much, the winds will rise into the upper part of your body, causing problems. For that reason the spine should be neither extended too straight nor hunched; it should be erect with a slight inward curvature.

Your neck should not be extended too much. If it is too bent, it will be difficult to breathe. Thus you should tuck your chin very slightly.

Let your right and left shoulders settle naturally, but that doesn't mean the armpits, which should be open. The reason is that there is a cavity for dullness in the armpits, and that cavity should not be covered. There should be room for the air to move, which will help prevent dullness from developing.

Let the eyes and nose rest naturally. Do not look either too far away or too close, which is uncomfortable. Look naturally into the space straight in front of yourself.

There are many points about the posture, of which I have explained the main ones very briefly. You may have studied these already.

Visualizing the Sources of Refuge

The text to recite begins:

> Before me in the sky is the Guru Vajradhara,
> Surrounded by the gurus of the lineage of meaning and blessings
> And gurus with whom I have dharmic connections of faith.
> In front are the yidams, to the right are the buddhas.
> All are surrounded by ocean-like retinues of their own kind.

> My mothers, sentient beings, and I stand together
> As the sources of refuge gaze down upon us.
> One-pointedly, we go for refuge and arouse bodhichitta.

First of all, when it says, "Before me in the sky," that means we do not need to raise our eyes and look up, nor do we need to lower our gaze and look down. We look straight ahead, without glancing to the right or left. When we stand up to prostrate and put our joined hands to the top of our head, we make a shadow. It is said that we visualize the field of refuge as being far enough away that our shadow does not touch it.

In the center of the field of refuge, you should visualize a jeweled throne supported by lions. It is okay for you to visualize as many or as few lions as you want. If you visualize four lions, they symbolize the four fearlessnesses.[1] If you visualize eight, they symbolize the eight qualities of mastery,[2] so visualizing eight is also fine. In any case, the lions should not be like drawings: they are real, three-dimensional, full-bodied lions, alive and trembling with breath. Their eyes are wide open and lined with red veins. Their claws are sharp. They are vivacious and glorious, with waving tails and manes. In any case you should visualize magnificent, living lions. It is fine to visualize either African lions or lions such as those drawn by Tibetans. The main thing is to visualize four or eight such lions to symbolize either the four fearlessnesses or the eight qualities of mastery.

On the lions' backs there is a throne, which should be square. There are many deities, so if you visualize a throne that is too small, you might feel they could not all fit. But if the throne is too high or too wide, no one could see it. If it is too large, we might not be able to get our minds around it.

So how big should it be? When we look at it, it is square, but when we want to see what size it actually is, we should visualize it as being immeasurable. For example, if we look from here off to the Bodhgaya Mahabodhi Temple in the distance, it seems as if it would fit in our hand. But when we go there and look at it, it is huge and seems endless. In the same way, when we look at the field of refuge from afar, it is in front of us. When we look for its edges, we cannot find any edges. That is how we should think about and visualize it.

As a symbol of the completion of the two accumulations, the throne is studded with gems and decorated with jewel ornaments. You can imagine it however you like, but it should be made of various precious things.

In the middle of that large throne there is another, smaller throne supported by lions. On top of that there is a lotus, which represents being unstained by the faults of samsara. On top of that, visualize that there is a sun and moon seat, which symbolizes either relative and ultimate wisdom or means and wisdom. Visualize Vajradhara seated on top of those.

How should we visualize the lama Vajradhara? Whom do we visualize? In the Geluk tradition, the *Offerings to the Gurus* ceremony is considered extremely important, because the principal figure of the field of refuge is visualized as having four traits: he or she is one's own kind root lama and he or she is also simultaneously Tsongkhapa Lobsang Drakpa, the Buddha Shakyamuni, and the Vajrayana teacher Vajradhara. This is what is called "having the four traits." The principal figure of the field of refuge must have these four qualities.

The way I think about it, generally in our Kagyu practice, we consider that our own individual root lama is the most important for our own individual practice, and we visualize that lama in the form of Vajradhara as the principal figure of the field of refuge. There is nothing wrong with this, and there are many reasons for it, such as that we can receive the blessings more quickly and easily from our root lama. This is how it is in the context of our own individual meditation practice.

However, in terms of the Karma Kagyu in general and Buddhism overall, this leaves a few traits that still need to be fulfilled. If we talk about the teachings of the Karma Kamtsang in particular, the Karmapa is the head of the lineage and the source of the teachings. For all of us practitioners who follow him, the founder of our lineage is the Karmapa—the Karmapa is like the father of the Karma Kamtsang. This is something we need to remember whenever we do any practice. If we do not, the Kamtsang teachings may decline somewhat. The way I see it, without practicing in this way, we will not be able to cooperate and progress together. It is like what happens among some Chinese students: it is as if they think that their own master is the most important and basically do not accept any others. We must not be like that. Here the main figure should be your own kind root lama and also the Karmapa, because this is a practice of the Karma Kamtsang tradition.

Shakyamuni Buddha is the founder of Buddhism, so if we were not to value him, we would not qualify as Buddhists. Therefore, the main figure is also the Teacher Shakyamuni. Similarly, the master of the Vajrayana teachings is Vajradhara, so it should also be Vajradhara. I feel that visualizing the main figure as having these four traits is good in terms of Buddhism in general, in terms of the specific teachings of the Karma Kamtsang, and in terms of our own practice. This is not a question of me trying to elevate the Karmapa into a higher position just because I have the name Karmapa.

To the right and left as well as in front and behind the principal figure are the lamas of the Kamtsang lineage of the realization of Dharma. There are also the lamas of the lineage of practice, who may not have developed realization but who do hold the lineage of practice. Likewise there are all the lamas, however many they may be, with whom you have made a Dharma connection or for whom you have developed faith even if you do not have a Dharma connection. Visualize these lamas to the right, left, front, and back, however you like, and imagine that they are all facing you.

In front of the lamas, visualize whichever yidam deities you feel devotion for. In terms of this lineage, the main deity to visualize is the yidam Vajrayogini. To the right are all the buddhas, with Buddha Shakyamuni foremost among them.

In the back is the genuine Dharma. The main aspect of Dharma is scripture and realization, or the truths of cessation and the path. We visualize this all in the form of scriptures or books. To the left is the Sangha of bodhisattvas who dwell on the high levels, surrounded by others of the same type. This is the same as in the case of the buddhas, who are surrounded by other buddhas similar to themselves. Think that the main bodhisattvas are the principal figures and that they are surrounded by all the other bodhisattvas.

The direction they are gazing is downward, but when we say they gaze down, that does not mean directly beneath the sources of refuge. It is below and in front of them, where we visualize ourselves and all sentient beings who are as limitless as space, with ourselves foremost among them. There are many different beings, including humans and animals, and there are two ways to visualize them: you can visualize them in their own forms, or alternatively you can visualize them all in human form. Either way is fine. If you visualize them in their own forms, it is easy to imagine the suffering and feelings that each of these beings experiences. If you visualize them as humans, it creates a good connection for them to be born as intelligent humans with leisures or riches. It does not matter which of the two you visualize.

You yourself are in the center of all sentient beings. Sometimes it is said that you should visualize your enemies in front of you, your father and mother on your right and left, and all other sentient beings behind you. It is fine to visualize it in that way, but it is also okay not to. The main thing is that you are in the middle. But it is not as if you pushed and shoved to get to the middle of a crowd. It's like being on the top of a high hill and being able to see the whole area around when you look down. You are in the middle, but when you look around, all sentient beings can fit within your field of vision and in front of the sources of refuge. Otherwise, when you are focusing on the visualization and prostrating, you might wonder whether those who are behind you are prostrating or not. People often think this. So you should visualize that you yourself are in the center and that when you look around, you can see all sentient beings. Since you are imagining that you are leading them all in going for refuge and developing bodhichitta, mentally it is easier if you can see them all.

If your room is very small, when you visualize a lot of people there is the problem that they do not all fit inside your room. For example, in a big hall like this one, we think a lot of people will fit, but if we are doing our practice or the ngondro meditation in a small room, we look a bit to the right and a bit to the left and see that they won't all fit.

Usually we make so much use of our five senses that it seems to us that whatever is in our thoughts has to exist on the outside. But it is not like that: Things that we think of do not need to exist on the outside. For instance, when we think, "Everyone is here," while practicing, we might then think, "This might just work," or we might think, "Is everyone going to fit in here?" Sometimes we think they won't all fit. When we look with our eyes or use our five senses, we think that there is a limit from a point over here to a point over there, so what we have to imagine does not come easily to the five senses. Therefore when you practice, you should not look at the house, walls, or pillars. If you look with your eyes and see that not everyone will fit, it will just get worse. Relax your mind. Even if you have a tiny house, you can still have a dream with a lot of people in it. Take that as an example and do not make your five senses the judge—make your imagination the judge instead. If you think about it this way, the visualization will be easier.

In this practice, there are five jewels. The traditional ngondro texts normally include the jewel of the wisdom dharma protectors, which makes six jewels. However, the text I used as the basis for this practice leaves out the dharma protectors and has only five jewels. Therefore I did the same, so there are only five kinds of jewels here. The wisdom dharma protectors are left out and do not appear in the field of refuge. The reason for this is that although in ultimate terms it is appropriate to rely on the wisdom dharma protectors as a source of refuge, in terms of their form or the way they manifest, the dharma protectors appear as guardian servants and protectors of yogis, not as a source of refuge. This is why the dharma protectors are visualized as protectors but not as sources of refuge in the field of refuge, and it is why they are not included here. It is permissible to visualize the dharma protectors outside the field of refuge.

The Meaning of Refuge

Now I will briefly explain refuge. When we say, "going for refuge," there are two main words here: *going* and *refuge*. *Refuge* means an infallible support. *Going* indicates that when we are stricken with some sort of fear, we look for someone who can protect us and we follow them. Thus we first look for a refuge, and then we ask for protection.

There are two causes for going for refuge: fear and faith. If we are fearful and afraid of the pervasive suffering of formation and the other types of suffering, we naturally feel a wish to go for refuge. If we feel faith when we perceive or know the qualities of the Three Jewels and that they can protect us, we naturally develop the wish to rely upon them as our refuge. Thus both fear and faith are indispensable for looking for refuge or for relying on a source of refuge. However, fear merely encourages us to look for a source of refuge; the actual cause of going for refuge is faith. I wonder whether going for refuge out of dread and fear is authentically going for refuge.

There are three sources of refuge: the Buddha, Dharma, and Sangha. We think of the Buddha as the teacher who shows us the path and then take refuge in him. We perceive the Dharma as the champion that protects us from misdeeds and terrifying situations and then take refuge in it. Similarly, we think of the Sangha as our companions in accomplishing the path and then we go for refuge in it. But even if we have taken refuge in the Buddha, unless we see the Dharma as that which actually removes our suffering and practice it, we will not gain liberation. In the same way, even if we take refuge in the Dharma and begin to practice, unless we have the companionship of the Sangha or of an authentic spiritual friend, we will be deluded from the start and unable to distinguish what we should take up from what we should give up. This is why it is critical that to have all three when we go for refuge.

We need to know the benefits of going for refuge and the faults of not doing so. Of all the many benefits of going for refuge, the greatest for ordinary individuals is that once we have taken refuge in the Three Jewels, each and every act we perform while thinking of the Three Jewels becomes a cause for awakening to buddhahood. This happens however we act—even if we do not have a virtuous motivation or good intent—simply because of the strength of the source of refuge. Sometimes we think that we ought to develop a genuinely pure, wholesome motivation, but then find it difficult. Yet the power of the sources of refuge gives us strength without requiring much effort from our own side, and this increases our confidence.

The Precepts of Refuge

Next I will explain the precepts of going for refuge. It is necessary to discuss the precepts after talking about refuge. Perhaps you can only determine whether going for refuge is appropriate for you after you have learned what it requires of you. Once you know that, you can decide whether you need to take action.

There are two types of precepts for the refuge vow: the specific precepts, and the general. First are the specific precepts, of which there are two kinds: the things to avoid and the things to do. The things to avoid are explained first, and then the things to do. This is because there are so many things we ordinary individuals first need to stop doing, whereas the things we need to do are part of what we need to accomplish. This is why the things we need to do are presented second, and the things we need to avoid are explained first.

There are three things that we need to avoid. First, having gone for refuge to the Buddha, do not take refuge in the worldly gods. Second, having gone for refuge to the Dharma, do not harm other sentient beings. Third, having gone for refuge to the Sangha, do not keep company with negative friends.

The main reason for saying, "Having gone for refuge to the Buddha, do not take refuge in worldly gods," comes down to this: Ultimately going for refuge in the Buddha and going for refuge in general itself entails at the very least fear of the pervasive suffering of formation or of experiencing the suffering of the lower realms in future lives. This is the minimum sort of fear that is necessary. Taking refuge merely out of apprehension of the difficulties and dangers of this life is not authentically going for refuge.

Therefore, if we want to enjoy the sensory pleasures of this life, we would need to rely on the worldly gods. But since the worldly gods themselves have no control over lifetimes other than this, relying on them is pointless. Thus once we have gone for refuge in the Buddha, we do not go for refuge to worldly gods. It mainly comes down to ourselves:

> We are our own protectors—
> Who else could be our protector?

What is important is to use our own capacities to practice the Dharma, making ourselves able to help our own selves. What this seems to be saying is that worshipping someone else is not important.

I don't know how some of you came up with this idea, but when we say in this context that we should be afraid of suffering, some people think that first we should think about suffering and then create some huge suffering— only then can we remember it. Although you might conceive of it like this, that is not what it is actually like. If it were, Buddhism would be a religion of suffering—we would only meditate on impermanence and suffering. When we say in this context that we should be afraid of suffering, that does not mean that we need to experience the feeling of suffering. It means that we need to be able to explain what suffering is; we need to be able to gain an understanding of it. It does not mean that you have to suffer or create suffering for yourselves.

When we say, "Having gone for refuge to the Dharma, do not harm other sentient beings," not harming others is only explaining it from one perspective. The main thing we need to do is gain the ability to give up all of the afflictions and obscurations that conflict with the truths of cessation and the path, in all our actions with our bodies, speech, and minds. "Not harming" does not just mean do not harm someone else. Basically, as long as the causes of harm—the three poisons of the afflictions—are present, at any given time we are close to causing harm—harm can possibly occur. This is such a frightening situation that it would not be right not to eliminate the causes themselves. If you had a nuclear bomb, for instance, although you might say you would not use it and would put it aside, there would be the danger it could go off at any time. Similarly, our bombs are the three poisonous afflictions in our own beings. Thus we are in an extremely dangerous situation.

When we say, "Having gone for refuge to the Sangha, do not keep company with negative friends," the phrase "negative friends" means people who spoil even our slightest virtuous thoughts. We need to be careful about such people. Some of us might understand negative friends to mean people who create a huge problem or shake us up so greatly that we think they have done something terrible. We might not pay much attention to all the little things that preceded it. But these things begin small and then get big. Therefore you should avoid those negative friends who prevent you from developing even tiny virtuous wishes.

That completes the things you should avoid. Although the explanation of things you should do usually comes next, no particular explanation is necessary. These are, however, things that you need to do.[3]

Taking Refuge

Now it is time to take the refuge vows. Before taking the refuge vow, it has all been just words, but when we take the vow, it should not be merely words: if we are really and truly saying the words, they should be meaningful and they should be said with feeling. To bring about this feeling, take what is already present within your being and combine it with the refuge vow. If you combine taking refuge with the Dharma that is present within you right now, I think it will have feeling.

If we can't find the Buddha whom we are taking refuge in, there's no way we can take refuge. When we look to see where there might be a buddha, we might look for someone who matches what the Buddha described as a buddha—someone who has extinguished all faults and who has all the qualities—but nowadays there isn't really anyone who has extinguished all faults and who has all the qualities. But there is the lama present before us—the spiritual friend to whom we are connected, who teaches us the Dharma and shows us the path—so we make the lama the Buddha's representative and think of them as a buddha.

But the spiritual friend is just someone for us to follow; we can't take the spiritual friend and whack the afflictions over the head with him. What we can use to hit the afflictions over the head is the Dharma. There are many things that we can say about the Dharma, although I have already explained the main points. At this point we do have subtle virtuous thoughts present within ourselves. Those might be faith, devotion, loving-kindness, or other such thoughts. Additionally, we instinctively had virtuous thoughts when we were children. We should remember all these thoughts now and evoke them especially. We should think that because of them we can start to practice and that because of them we are going to embark upon all the paths.

In my case, for example, I remember what it was like when I was four or five years old. Since I was a nomad, my family slaughtered animals. When an animal was killed, I naturally felt compassion or something like it, and the feeling was strong and intense. That was when I was four or five, but now I am getting into my twenties. I have read many books and occasionally done a bit of practice here and there, yet I have never since felt any compassion that could rival what I felt when I was little. This is why calling the qualities and love that we innately have to mind and bringing them into our Dharma practice is so much better than hundreds or thousands of conceptually fabricated practices.

Many of you have Dharma friends, but usually you only think about the lama and do not particularly pay any attention to your Dharma friends. Yet you should keep your Dharma friends in mind, and consider how you can create Dharma connections with one another and develop those Dharma connections through harmonious *samaya* commitments with one another. Considering this, you should rely upon each other. This is how you should think of the Three Jewels as you go for refuge today.

After having given you the refuge vows, I have a hope for all of you. Of course it is important for you to keep all the precepts I explained as well as you can—that is generally just how it is done. What I have to say from my own part is that I have no particular hope that now that I have given you the refuge vow, you will do your practice so well that in the future you will be able to perform great miracles, awaken to buddhahood, grow an ushnisha on your head, and have wheel designs on the soles of your feet. It is of course good if that happens, but I have no specific expectation of that. If I had such expectations, I should hope for the same for myself, but I haven't grown anything yet. The main point is that on this earth, communities are extremely important. If communities act in negative ways toward each other, it harms the entire earth. If communities act well toward each other and do good things, it brings good things to the whole world. Now that you have gathered here and I have given you the refuge vow, the main thing for all of you is that you take greater responsibility for this world. I hope that you develop more courage to work for happiness in the world, and that when your courage increases, all the particular intentions you now have for this world do not just remain mere thoughts but can really and truly be demonstrably shown on this earth. Do as much as you can as an individual to train in altruism and loving-kindness, and then do what you can to bring happiness from the small scale of within your family up to the larger scale of society in general and to all beings in this world. This is what I personally hope of you now that I have given you the refuge vows.

Generating Bodhichitta

The word *bodhichitta* means the "mind of enlightenment." It does not mean the "mouth of enlightenment," thus we need to develop the mental attitude of bodhichitta. You should each for your own part put effort into it. Generally, everyone has the seeds of loving-kindness, compassion, and bodhichitta. We just need to increase them—we don't have to buy them new. So please be persistent on your own part and meditate on the precious mind of enlightenment.

Prostrations

There are three types of prostration: mental prostrations, verbal prostrations, and physical prostrations. Joining your hands and bowing your head is a physical prostration, singing praises is a verbal prostration, and mentally recalling qualities and developing faith is a mental prostration. You might think that feeling faith in your mind and reciting praises must not be prostrating—that a prostration has to involve physically bowing and scraping. But this is not so, because the Sanskrit word for prostration, *namo*, means to pay respect as well as prostrate.

There is a story about this. Somewhere in China in 1925, there was a butcher who had slaughtered many animals and then passed away. At the time of his death, he felt faith in the Buddha and raised one of his hands out of respect. One night nine months later, all of his family members had the same dream. They dreamt that the next day a piglet would be born in their neighbor's pigsty with one human hand. In the dream, the piglet begged, "Please protect me." As in the dream, the next day such a piglet was born. When they saw it had actually occurred as they had dreamt, the family bought the piglet and released it in a monastery that had an area set aside for animals whose lives had been saved. This is probably the benefit of raising a single hand in respect. If raising a single hand has that much benefit, joining both hands must have a much greater benefit. This has a significant meaning.

According to the sutras, the best way to gather the accumulations is the seven-branch practice, and prostrating is performing all seven branches. Paying respect with body, speech, and mind is prostration. Pleasing the buddhas is offering. Purifying one's misdeeds, obscurations, wrongs, and downfalls through the power of support—one of the four powers of the antidote—is confessing. Feeling happy about such purification of misdeeds and so forth is rejoicing. This becomes a cause for the buddhas and bodhisattvas to promise to turn the wheel of Dharma and stay longer in this world realm, thus it is a request to turn the wheel of Dharma and a supplication not to pass into nirvana. Dedicating this virtue to achieving buddhahood is the dedication.

Next is how to prostrate, starting with how to join your hands: Touch your fingertips together but leave space between the centers of your hands so that they do not touch. Then insert your thumbs between the hands. Your hands should have the shape of a lotus blossom that has not yet opened but is just about to bloom. Leaving the empty space in the center represents the dharmakaya. The shape represents the form kayas. The right and left hands represent means and wisdom—at least when we act virtuously. If we act un virtuously, they might represent maras and obstructors! By joining these two representations of means and wisdom, we create the auspicious connection for the path to arise where it has not arisen, never weaken where it has arisen, and continue to grow and develop without weakening, through the union of means and wisdom.

Once we have joined our palms, we touch them first to our forehead. Then we place them at the level of the throat, and then we touch them to our heart. This represents the qualities of the buddhas' three places and the purification of the obscurations of the three gates.[4] Doing this is a cause for purifying the obscurations.

When you do the refuge practice in the future, you are going to have to prostrate, and when you prostrate, you will generally have to do full prostrations. There are also many other types of prostrations, such as half prostrations—prostrations where the five points touch the ground.[5] Full prostrations mainly appear in vajrayana instructions, whereas the half prostration, also called the prostration of the fivefold mandala, is the usual type of Buddhist prostration. It is okay to do full prostrations, and it is also okay to do half prostrations. Alternatively, if your knees are bad, it is permissible to kneel, touch your hands to the three places, and then touch your head to the floor. You don't have to get up but can prostrate while kneeling.

Usually it is said that one should do a few hundred thousand prostrations. But many foreigners complain a lot when they do prostrations—they say that their back hurts or their knees hurt. Prostrating is good, but if trying to do a hundred thousand becomes a huge hassle and causes great difficulties, it is no longer Dharma practice. Since this is a ngondro practice that I wrote, when you practice, you can decrease the number a bit. You do not absolutely have to do one hundred thousand prostrations. The minimum is one thousand or ten thousand, or perhaps fifty thousand. Full prostrations are fine, and half prostrations are also fine. If you are able to do more, don't limit yourself to a hundred thousand; it is also fine to do two hundred thousand. But even if you reduce the number of prostrations, you still must recite the refuge prayer at least one hundred thousand times.

The most important thing to understand about prostrations is that a prostration is an expression or convention of body and speech that can show our respect. If doing this can demonstrate pure action of the three gates, it is a prostration. Otherwise it is not a prostration. If the prostrations we do fulfill that criterion, it does not matter how many times we prostrate. We can still gather the accumulations, and we have accomplished the primary purpose. In Tibet, prostrations can be scary—when you see them, they seem terrifying. Prostrations should not be like that; they should be an expression of faith.

The Vajrasattva Practice

When we speak about purifying misdeeds, we talk about the four powers: the power of support, the power of regret, the power of resolve, and the power of acting on the antidote. I think that the easiest of these is the power of support, because the power of support is to rely on the precious Three Jewels or the field of merit. Therefore, even if our own intentions or actions do not quite measure up, that on which we are relying—the power of support—helps us greatly. For instance, when we confess misdeeds, even if our actual intent and action in making the confession do not measure up, taking the Three Jewels as a support while making confessions will make purifying our misdeeds faster and easier, through the power of the compassion of the Three Jewels.

When we talk about confessing misdeeds, many people think that when we say, "confess misdeeds," it means, "I killed a bug in the past and now I need to confess it." Or perhaps it is, "I killed a horse and have to confess that misdeed," or even, "I murdered someone and have to confess that." That is excellent, but there is something even more important than that. If we first make a commitment or form a great hope and then later do some wrong that violates it, that is a far graver harm. Generally killing horses or people is wrong and confessing it is good. But performing a misdeed that violates a strong commitment or great hope we have made mentally brings greater harm upon ourselves.

If someone were to kill some insects incidentally—for instance, if a bug were crawling here and they squashed and killed it with their hands or feet—there would not be any immediate harm to them. The suffering that is its karmic ripening does not immediately occur. It is, of course, wrong, but it does not immediately lead to any great harm to them. This is because when we kill an insect, we do it in passing without a long period of advance preparation or premeditation. Because of the motivation, it does not bring us much harm. We frequently kill many bugs underfoot, but we don't particularly feel as if we were killing.

However, if we make a firm commitment and form a strong hope, and then perform a wrong or other act that contradicts it, the harm it brings us is greater. The reason for this is that commitments and hopes are phenomena that can stay with us for a long time, and therefore doing something that violates them is more harmful to us. Thus it is even more important to confess wrongs that contradict the three vows than to confess misdeeds such as killing sentient beings.

For this reason, when we say that a wrong is either grave or minor, it is not as if there were someone pretending to be a buddha and ranking our misdeeds on some scale, saying, "That wrong you committed is serious, but this one is not." What we need to look at to determine whether a wrong is serious or minor is how harmful it is to our being and whether or not it creates great damage in our mind stream. If something you have done harms your mind greatly or has a big impact on you, then that is probably a very serious wrong. If it does not have a strong negative effect on your mind, produce an intense feeling, or make a strong impact on you, then you have committed a wrong, but I think it is a minor wrong.

What is the main thing we need to know when confessing our misdeeds? If we have done some specific misdeed and confess it in particular, that is good. It is good to specifically remember the wrongs we have done and confess them. But when we confess misdeeds, it is not necessary to remember each and every instance and confess each individually. It is better to do an overall confession of all the misdeeds we have done under the influence of the three poisons of the afflictions from beginningless time up to now. The reason is that it would be extremely difficult to specify each and every misdeed and confess them all individually. With me, for example, I don't remember committing any particularly serious wrong when I was little, but I did do many small wrongs, none of which I remember. We are all the same: we have done many wrongs but do not remember them. However, none of the wrongs we have done have not been mixed with the three poisons of the afflictions, so if we confess all the wrongs that we have committed when motivated by the three poisons, we will be able to confess all our misdeeds whether we remember them or not.

There are primarily three conditions that lead to committing misdeeds. The one that is like the boss is delusion, and the two henchmen are greed and hatred. This is because delusion permeates all of the afflictions. From the delusion of not knowing, we perceive things incorrectly and then regard them inappropriately. This is why delusion permeates all the afflictions just as the sense of touch permeates the body. "Just like the sense of touch in the body" it is said. That is the reason why delusion is said to be like the boss. When we say that greed and hatred are like henchmen, although there are many afflictions under the control of delusion, the primary ones—the ones that really and truly have power and that we mainly employ—are greed and hatred. That is why they are said to be like henchmen. It is impossible that there is any wrong we commit that did not happen because of either greed or hatred.

When we classify the misdeeds in terms of our motivation, there are three types: those committed primarily under the power of the affliction of delusion, those committed under the power of the affliction of hatred, and those committed under the power of the affliction of greed. If we see any act performed under the influence of the afflictions as revolting and confess it, we can confess and purify all our misdeeds.

If we explain our actions or karma in terms of what we use to commit them, there are three types: actions of body, of speech, and of mind. Any act we do must be performed with either body, speech, or mind. Any misdeed we commit is thus done with body, speech, or mind.

If we classify acts in terms of how they are committed, there are three types: those we perform ourselves, those we have someone else do, and those that we rejoice in having been done. Those we perform are acts that we actually do ourselves. Those we have someone else do are those that we get someone else to do instead of doing ourselves. These are more harmful. We pretend that we have not done anything wrong, but if we have told someone else to do it, then we have made two people accumulate wrongdoing, haven't we? That is a graver wrong. When someone else has committed a misdeed and we think, "What a guy! Way to go!" or "Well done!" and rejoice in that, the strength of that thought creates a misdeed for us as well. How does this misdeed occur? It is not as if a portion of the misdeed committed by the other is allotted to us or we accrue some interest from it. We get the whole misdeed or the entire wrong. An individual who rejoices in someone else's misdeed incurs the entire negativity; the negativity is not divided into portions and each person gets one part. Thus it is the same as performing the misdeed oneself.

Visualizing Vajrasattva

Before you recite the Vajrasattva liturgy, you should recite the entire refuge practice. Refuge and bodhichitta are as I have already described, but they do not need to be done for four sessions daily. However, if you are specifically doing the Vajrasattva practice on its own, you need to recite refuge and bodhichitta. After you go for refuge and develop bodhichitta well, then you should recite the Vajrasattva meditation, which begins

> Above the crown of my head, on a lotus-moon seat,
> Is Guru Vajrasattva, white in color, adorned with ornaments,
> With one face and two arms,
> Holding a vajra with his right hand and a bell with his left, and seated
>   in vajra posture.

When it says, "Above the crown of my head," you should visualize yourself as your normal self, the ordinary individual that you currently are. You do not need to visualize yourself as any deity. The reason for this is that it is easier to remember the wrongs or misdeeds that you have committed if you see yourself as a normal person. Since ordinary individuals are faulty by nature, we view ourselves as such to make it easier to remember our wrongs. You should see yourself as your ordinary self who has committed all sorts of wrongs.

Visualize that about ten inches above the crown of your head in the sky there is an eight-petaled lotus flower, white in color, symbolizing being unstained by the faults of samsara. Imagine that on that seat there is a full moon—a perfectly round moon—which is by nature relative bodhichitta. This moon disk looks like the moon we see when we look up from the earth. That is how you should picture it. You should not see it as the dark sphere resembling an overbaked roll we see in pictures that scientists have taken of the moon from up close. You should visualize it as white and radiant. To explain it in detail, it is the color white because relative bodhichitta is the source of all white, positive, virtuous phenomena. It is full and whole because it is directed equally toward all sentient beings without any sense of closeness or distance. Because it quells the flames of the selfish attention that thinks there is no one other than oneself, it is cool. Since it is excellent benefit for others, it is radiant. That is how we should visualize it.

Then visualize the body of Vajrasattva. There is not any meditation on letters or seed syllables; the visualization is instantaneous. You should immediately picture Vajrasattva's body as complete.

I should probably explain the reason why he is called Vajrasattva. The word *vajra* is explained as having many different aspects and many different meanings in Sanskrit, but the main meaning is "extremely firm and stable": the Buddha's body is nondual wisdom and is invincible by the four maras. Since Vajrasattva has that nature, he is called *vajra*. Then the word *sattva* or "heroic being" means that he manifests the state of the indivisible wisdom and kaya that has transcended even the subtlest of cognitive obscurations as well as the slightest afflictive obscurations. But for the sake of taming sentient beings, he appears in the form body of a sambhogakaya. Since he is a being who acts for the benefit of sentient beings without ever getting discouraged, he is called a *sattva*.

When it says, "Vajrasattva, white in color, adorned with ornaments," the reason his body is white in color is because of the extremely subtle wind of pristine wisdom. This wind is white in color, so we visualize him as white.

It is said that Vajrasattva is "peaceful and smiling." It is important to visualize that he has a peaceful and smiling expression. Otherwise we might think of him as immobile like a statue, and there would not be any feeling to our meditation. But if we visualize him as having a smiling and laughing expression, we get the feeling that we are really seeing him. You should visualize that he is smiling at you, the yogi, in particular.

There are two reasons why he is smiling and laughing. The first is to represent how rare this is. Normally it is extremely difficult to practice any Dharma such as this and confess misdeeds, accomplish virtue, and contemplate in this way. But now in his presence you yourself are trying to do something to eliminate your misdeeds and accomplish virtue. This is very rare, so he is smiling in a manner that indicates that he is pleased. That is the reason to visualize him as smiling at you.

He is also laughing in an encouraging manner. He is not laughing because he is pleased—we don't have any qualities that would please him. Instead, it is like a mother who has only one child who never listens to her and is always rowdy. At first she talks to him, but he does not pay attention. Spanking him would not be right, but there is nothing else she can do, so she just laughs. It is similar with us: our minds mainly go in an unvirtuous, negative direction and hardly ever go in a positive, virtuous direction, so there is not much Vajrasattva can do but sit there laughing. This is to encourage us to make real effort.

Vajrasattva has two hands. In his right hand there is a five-pointed vajra and in his left, a bell. You should visualize that he is holding the vajra up to his heart and resting the bell on his hip. He is also sitting in the vajra posture.

Visualize that there is a moon disk in his heart. On it there is a letter HUM, which is the size of a person, although it is small if you look at it from afar.

You may visualize it either the size of a thumb or the size of a person, whichever is easier for you.

If you focus your attention on him and pray, you might have a genuine feeling that your misdeeds are being purified, or your prayer might be especially strong. Because of this, a stream of nectar then flows down from his body. It is not as if he is sweating—it would be bizarre if a stream of sweat were to trickle down. Actually, his body is not like a physical body of flesh and blood. It is clear and unclouded like a crystal or a rainbow, so you should think that it is a stream of amrita nectar that flows from his body.

The nectar flows from the toe of his right foot and enters you through the fontanelle in the crown of your head. It fills the entire inside of your body, and all your misdeeds and obscurations dissolve into the ground below like ink or soot. The stream of nectar fills you with all the qualities and there is nothing left in your being that is a misdeed of speech or that oppresses your mind with sorrow. You should think that you have created dignity in your mind, that you have grasped courage and taken control over your mind.

There are many visualizations you could do, of light radiating and purifying your misdeeds or of the flow of the stream of nectar, but the visualization of the nectar flowing is probably the easiest of these to do. Normally we think that we can wash away all our dirt when we take a bath, right? But if we turn on a light, it only seems to make more dust and we don't think that it particularly cleanses the dirt from our bodies. In this context as well, if we think that there is nectar or liquid flowing down, we can really believe that we have been purified. At this point, do the visualization well, but do not particularly focus on the visualization while reciting the mantra. This mantra is what you should recite one-hundred thousand times.

Confessing and Resolving

Next, confess your past negative actions and vow not to perform them again:

> Noble ones who know and see everything, think of us.
> Since beginningless time,
> Under the power of the three poisons,
> We have transgressed the three vows and the victors' commands
> In body, speech, and mind.
> We admit and confess these downfalls and misdeeds
> And promise not to do them again—may we not experience their results.

You have been meditating that the main figure Vajrasattva, inseparable from our lama Vajradhara, is above the crown of your head. You should take him as the principal witness and then also think of the bodhisattvas and lineage lamas. It is not really necessary to imagine them to be witnesses as well—you should just think they are present. Then confess all that you have done from beginningless time in any of the three times that transgresses the commands of the Buddha. After confessing what you have done in the past, the main thing is to vow not to do such acts again. If you do not actually hold to that vow, you will once again commit the wrong of lying. You will have the wrong of first having done a misdeed and the additional wrong of lying, so you need to be careful.

Because you have confessed your misdeeds and vowed not to commit them again, Vajrasattva is pleased and says, "You have been completely purified," to inspire you, and then melts into light. When it says in the text that he "is pleased," that means that he is truly happy with you. It is as if he is pleased and says, "You've done really well. You have accomplished something. That's good."

When we say "Vajrasattva" here, generally our obscurations are purified through the appearance of our own innate pristine wisdom as the deity. This is what we imagine. We need to purify our misdeeds through our practice. There really isn't any deity who descends and blesses us so that we are free of misdeeds. The buddhas and bodhisattvas are like examples, and when we take them as examples and imagine them, our own corresponding inherent wisdom and means arise as the male and female deities. This then becomes an excellent way to purify our misdeeds. It's not anything else. It would be really difficult for some god to come, sprinkle water on us, and purify our negativity. If that were possible, we all would have been purified long ago. The most important thing is that complete purification comes about by our keeping our minds on the visualization and bringing out the strength of wisdom and means. In this light, whether or not we are able to purify ourselves and how quickly that happens depend mainly upon us individually, as well as upon the blessings of the lineage.

Then Vajrasattva melts into light and dissolves into us. After that, rest evenly without altering your mind at all. Stopping the occurrence of the net of conceptuality and resting evenly in the unaltered nature just might be helpful for developing the ability to rest in mahamudra and for manifesting our inner pristine wisdom.

Mandala Offerings

I will explain mandala offerings briefly. First of all, there are said to be many types of merit, such as conditioned merit and unconditioned merit. It is extremely difficult for ordinary individuals to instill conditioned virtuous merit and unconditioned merit into their beings. Whatever phase we are in, whether the phase of ground, path, or fruition, a great deal of conditioned virtuous merit is needed. It is difficult for individuals who lack merit to even hear the words "path" and "Dharma," let alone develop the path within themselves. This is why we need to make the accumulation of merit within our beings complete, which we should do by making mandala offerings. It is for this reason that we do the mandala practice.

The sutras and tantras both talk about how to make mandala offerings. Generally, the word *mandala* is a Sanskrit word that means "to take the essence." Thus before we offer the mandala we need to identify what the essence is that we are taking. It is the result, the three kayas—the dharmakaya, sambhogakaya, and nirmanakaya. The method by which we take their essence is to continuously offer mandalas to the buddhas and bodhisattvas, which makes the obscurations in our beings become thinner and thinner and the qualities grow stronger and stronger. Ultimately we will manifest the state where all faults have been extinguished and all qualities gained. Then at last we will be able to take the essence.

Types of Mandalas

We need to know what materials mandala plates can be made of. There are three types of material: the best, the average, and the least. The best mandala plates are made of precious substances such as gold and silver. The middling are made of iron or copper, and the least are made of wood, clay, stone, and so forth.

Mandalas come in different shapes and colors. For example, pacifying mandalas are square, enriching are round, magnetizing are crescent-shaped, and mandalas for wrathful activity are triangular. Similarly, each of the different activities of pacifying, enriching, magnetizing, and destroying has its own color. There are also large, medium, and small-sized mandalas, but the minimum size it should be is twelve finger widths across. These are the physical characteristics of the mandalas that we can use.

When we offer mandalas, there are two types: the mandala of accomplishment and the mandala of offering. The mandala of accomplishment is set up as a representation, and the other mandala is used for actually making offerings. If all the sources of refuge mentioned here—the Buddha, Dharma, yidam, lamas, and Sangha—are present in your shrine room, it is not necessary to have a special mandala of accomplishment. But whether in actuality you have the mandala of accomplishment or not, you should visualize the sources of refuge on the base of the mandala as they are described above,[6] whichever type of mandala it may be. Then offer a seven-branch prayer in a way that moves you and with all the branches properly fulfilled.

Making the Offerings

When you offer one hundred thousand mandalas, the most important mandala is the offering mandala. You mainly make seven-heap mandala offerings on the offering mandala. To describe the seven-heap offerings, the mandala plate represents the golden ground of the earth, and on that ground is the golden earth anointed with fragrant scents, scattered with flowers, and completely circled with a ring of iron mountains around its perimeter. In the middle is the king of mountains, Mount Meru, surrounded by the four main continents in the four directions and also adorned by the sun and moon to its right and left. Visualize it as a pure land created by the intentions and aspirations of the buddhas. You should make this offering thinking that through the power of visualizing the offering, all wandering beings purify the stains of the defilements and enjoy the state of the four kayas within a realm that is utterly pure.

In terms of how the mandala is offered, we should first talk about what substances you should offer in the heaps. Offering medicinal herbs and other substances that sustain the body eliminates physical illnesses and brings long life. Offering precious stones and the like will cause your needs and wishes to be fulfilled and your purposes accomplished. Offering rice and grain that have been infused with a nice scent has the purpose of being able to elicit faith and generate renunciation in others. Medicinal herbs, grains, or any offering substances other than gems and precious stones for the offering piles get stale quickly, so you should not always use the same herbs and grain over and over again. You may, however, offer gems over and over again.

When you make the mandala offerings, keep some grain and gems in your left hand as you offer the mandalas. Holding the mandala plate with an empty hand does not create an auspicious connection. Then you can make the piles, whether of grain, medicinal substances, or gems, with your right hand. First wipe the mandala plate with your right wrist. In the Kamtsang tradition, we wipe it all the way around twice in a clockwise direction and once counterclockwise. Wiping it twice clockwise is most likely in terms of the outer classes of tantra, and wiping it once counterclockwise is in terms of the inner tantras. The ordinary custom is to wipe twice clockwise and once counterclockwise, but it is also okay to rub it either three times clockwise or three times counterclockwise.

Whether you wipe the plate clockwise or counterclockwise, the main thing is to do it with your right wrist. The reason is that the bodhichitta nerve is on the surface there. Because the bodhichitta nerve is there, this creates the interconnections that make it easier to purify afflictions, misdeeds, and obscurations and develop love and compassion. As you wipe the plate, you should think that this realm that you are taming is cleared of all rocks, mud, gravel, and any other impurities or faults. If you think that, it becomes the practice of purifying a realm described in the sutras on transcendent wisdom. It has all the elements of the practice of purifying a realm.

Hold some grains or gems in your right hand as you wipe the mandala plate, and when you are done place them in the center of the mandala plate. If you do not do that and leave the center empty, there might be the fault that you will be born in a realm that is pure but empty. Then you make the seven piles on the mandala. There is the king of mountains, Mount Meru, in the center and the four continents in the four directions, ornamented by the sun and moon. You should visualize these properly.

There are two different ways you consider the directions: You can consider east to be in front of yourself, or you can consider east to be in front of the mandala. Thus east is either the direction you are facing or the direction those to whom you are making the offering are facing. You consider the direction that those to whom you are giving offerings face as the east primarily to receive the blessing of the sources of refuge quickly. You consider the direction you are facing as the east to offer your body, speech, and mind. Either is acceptable.

In either case you should visualize Mount Meru in the center. These days there is a lot of discussion about whether or not Mount Meru exists, but whether something like the specific Mount Meru we visualize in our meditation absolutely has to exist is a different question. Some people visualize Mount Meru as square and some as round. There is no way it could exist exactly as each and every individual imagines it. Therefore the way you visualize it is not how it is. Instead, the main purpose is to broaden our attitude and actions so that what we call the four continents are purified of all their stains and impurities, so that they may become the pure realms of the buddhas.

Thus what is mentioned here are Mount Meru in the center, the four continents, the sun, and the moon. Alternatively, it would probably be fine to make a new seven-pile mandala with Asia in the east and America in the west and offer it, as long as you offer it properly. But before you made such an offering you would have to think a lot about it and then make something up, which would not be easy. What is essential here is that you transform your offering of Mount Meru and the four continents—that is, the whole universe—into a pure realm. This in turn will transfigure our attitude and vision into something tremendously vast.

For example, in Taiwan and China there is a lot of emphasis on the human pure realm. That human pure realm is precisely what we visualize here as the mandala. This is because a pure realm is not some fine, excellent place that already exists elsewhere. Pure realms come from purifying impure realms; a pure realm is not a place somewhere that has been excellent from the beginning. At first it has an impure nature, and it only becomes pure through being cleansed and purified. In the case of the pure realms of Amitabha and other buddhas, for instance, first the buddhas themselves were ordinary individuals, but through their training in purifying realms, gradually their place, country, and possessions were cleansed of impurities and stains and purified to the nature of pure wisdom. That is how pure realms such as Sukhavati were created, and we ourselves can also train in the same way.

Appendix A: The Sequence of Practice

Before doing this ngondro practice, one should ask for and receive instructions from a qualified master who can explain the details of each practice, many of which are not explained in this book. These practices should only be done under the direction of a qualified lama.

The Gyalwang Karmapa has said that one may recite these practices in either English or Tibetan. Some people find it beneficial to sometimes recite in English and sometimes in Tibetan, but always reciting in English or always reciting in Tibetan is also fine.

Going for Refuge and Giving Rise to Bodhichitta

1. Recite the Short Vajradhara Lineage Prayer with strong faith and devotion in the lamas of the lineage and your own root lama.
2. Recite the four ordinary foundations while contemplating their meaning.
3. Recite the *Brief Recitations for the Four Preliminary Practices*

from "Before me in the sky is the Guru Vajradhara..." up through the line "One-pointedly, we go for refuge and arouse bodhichitta." Visualize the field of refuge clearly.

4. Arise from your seat and begin to prostrate while reciting the refuge prayer as many times as you are able. Alternatively, you can prostrate for a while and then recite the refuge prayer for a while. You should recite the refuge prayer 100,000 times and do 100,000 prostrations. If you have knee or back ailments or any other condition that prevents you from doing 100,000 prostrations, you may do 10,000 or even 1,000 prostrations, but you must still recite the refuge prayer 100,000 times.

5. Then recite the bodhisattva vow "Until I reach enlightenment's essence..." three times.

6. Recite the verse "May precious and supreme bodhichitta..." once.

7. Dissolve the visualization and rest in meditation as long as you can.

8. Recite long life prayers for the Gyalwang Karmapa and your root guru, and then recite dedication and aspiration prayers such as prayers for rebirth in Sukhavati and the dedication of merit.

Vajrasattva Meditation

1. Recite the Short Vajradhara Lineage Prayer with strong faith and devotion in the lamas of the lineage and your own root lama.

2. Recite the four ordinary foundations while contemplating their meaning.

3. Do the Refuge and Bodhichitta practice, reciting the refuge prayer and prostrating three, seven, or twenty-one times, and reciting the bodhisattva vow three times. At the end of the refuge practice, dissolve the visualization and rest in meditation.

4. Begin Vajrasattva practice by reciting the verse "Above the crown of my head..." while visualizing Vajrasattva clearly above your head.

5. Recite the hundred-syllable mantra as many times as possible. You should count this mantra and recite it a total of 100,000 times.

6. When you have recited as many mantras as you are able, recite the verses that begin "Noble ones who know and see everything..."

7. Dissolve the visualization and rest in meditation.

8. Recite long life prayers for the Gyalwang Karmapa and your root guru, and then recite dedication and aspiration prayers such as prayers for rebirth in Sukhavati and the dedication of merit.

Mandala Offerings

1. Before you begin the practice, arrange the mandala of accomplishment on a shrine or other suitable place if there are not any representations of the Buddha, Dharma, Sangha, lamas, and yidam deities in your shrine room or the place where you practice.

2. Recite the Short Vajradhara Lineage Prayer with strong faith and devotion in the lamas of the lineage and your own root lama.

3. Recite the four ordinary foundations while contemplating their meaning.

4. Do the Refuge and Bodhichitta practice, reciting the refuge prayer and prostrating three, seven, or twenty-one times and reciting the bodhisattva vow three times.

5. Do the Vajrasattva practice, reciting the mantra three, seven, or twenty-one times.

6. Recite the seven branch prayer which begins "In the dharma expanse palace of Akanishtha…" with faith and devotion.

7. Recite the mandala offering stanza which begins "The earth is perfumed with scented water…" while offering seven-heap mandalas as many times as you are able. You should recite this prayer and offer the mandalas 100,000 times.

8. Recite the mantra IDAṂ GURU RATNA MAṆḌALA KAṂ NIRYĀTAYĀMI

9. Dissolve the visualization and rest in meditation.

10. Recite long life prayers for the Gyalwang Karmapa and your root guru, and then recite dedication and aspiration prayers such as prayers for rebirth in Sukhavati and the dedication of merit.

Appendix B: The Precepts of the Refuge Vow

The Three Things to Avoid:

1. Having gone for refuge in the Buddha, do not go for refuge in Brahma or any other worldly god.
2. Having gone for refuge in the Dharma, abandon harming sentient beings.
3. Having gone for refuge in the Sangha, avoid negative friends.

The Three Things to Do

1. Treat with respect all representations of the Buddha, even the small fragments of a clay figurine.
2. Treat with respect all representations of the Dharma, even just a single letter of a dharma text.
3. Treat with respect anyone who wears the saffron-color robes of a monastic.

The Five Common Precepts

1. Do not abandon the Three Jewels even at the cost of your life or for great material rewards.
2. The Three Jewels are just as important for your mind as food and drink are for your physical body, so do not cast them aside and look for another worldly method.
3. Always remembering the Three Jewels, offer the first portion of your food to them.
4. Since you know the benefits of going for refuge in the Three Jewels, always keep them in mind and encourage others to go for refuge.
5. Whatever direction you go, remember the Buddha of that direction and prostrate or pay homage to that Buddha. For instance, if you are in the west, you should try to remember Amitabha, the Buddha of the western pure land of Sukhavati.

Notes

1. The four fearlessnesses are qualities of the Buddha. The first fearlessness is knowing that he has perfect realization without any fear of dispute. The second is knowing that he has perfectly abandoned all faults without any fear of dispute. The third fearlessness is knowing that he can teach others what the impediments are, without any fear of dispute. The fourth fearlessness is knowing without any fear of dispute that he can teach the path to liberation.

2. The eight qualities or common siddhis shared with worldly meditators are: the qualities of a subtle body, of a coarse body, of lightness, of pervasiveness, of complete achievement, of complete brightness, of stability, and of all wishes being fulfilled.

3. See Appendix B for a list of all the precepts of the refuge vow.

4. The three gates are body, speech, and mind.

5. The five points touching the ground in a half prostration are the forehead, two hands, and two knees.

6. That is, as they are visualized during the refuge practice.

May all beings be happy!